PAZURGO

The Amazing New Word Puzzle

by **JEREMY L. GRAYBILL**

TUTTLE PUBLISHING
Tokyo • Rutland, Vermont • Singapore

Published by Tuttle Publishing, an imprint of Periplus Editions (HK) Ltd.

www.tuttlepublishing.com

Library of Congress Control Number: 2010922236

ISBN 978-0804841306

Distributed by

North America, Latin America & Europe
Tuttle Publishing
364 Innovation Drive
North Clarendon, VT 05759-9436 U.S.A.
Tel: 1 (802) 773-8930;
Fax: 1 (802) 773-6993
info@tuttlepublishing.com
www.tuttlepublishing.com

Japan
Tuttle Publishing
Yaekari Building, 3rd Floor
5-4-12 Osaki
Shinagawa-ku
Tokyo 141 0032
Tel: (81) 3 5437-0171
Fax: (81) 3 5437-0755
tuttle-sales@gol.com

Asia Pacific
Berkeley Books Pte. Ltd.
61 Tai Seng Avenue #02-12
Singapore 534167
Tel: (65) 6280-1330
Fax: (65) 6280-6290
inquiries@periplus.com.sg
www.periplus.com

15 14 13 12 11 10   10 9 8 7 6 5 4 3 2 1

Printed in Singapore

Puzzles Ranked by Difficulty

Step by Step Instructions

Puzzles

Difficulty: ★
Puzzle 2, 4 6, 8, 10

Difficulty: ★
Puzzle 13,15,17

Difficulty: ★★
Puzzle 1, 3, 5, 7, 9, 11

Difficulty: ★★
Puzzle 12, 14, 16, 18, 19, 20, 21, 22, 23, 24, 25, 26, 27, 28, 29, 30, 32

Difficulty: ★★★
Puzzle 31, 33, 34, 35, 36, 37, 38, 39, 40, 41, 42, 43, 44, 45, 46, 47, 48, 49, 50, 51, 52, 53, 54, 55, 56, 57, 58, 59, 60, 61, 62, 64, 66, 68, 70

Difficulty: ★★★
Puzzle 63, 65, 67, 69, 71, 72, 73, 74, 75, 76, 77, 78, 79, 81, 83

Difficulty: ★★★★
Puzzle 80, 82, 84, 85, 86, 87, 88, 89

Difficulty: ★★★★
Puzzle 90, 91, 92

Difficulty: ★★★★★
Puzzle 93, 95

Difficulty: ★★★★★
Puzzle 94, 96

Solutions to the Puzzles are located after Puzzle 96

Pazurgo® is a new, intuitive, and thrilling word puzzle which combines the trivia solving enjoyment of Crossword Puzzles with the fun of Word Searches, while also adding its own unique challenges and excitement. If you are a fan of Crossword Puzzles, Word Searches, Sudoku puzzles, or any other word and logic puzzles, give Pazurgo® a try, and I'm sure you will be very pleased. Pazurgo® is great for trips and vacations, for keeping the mind challenged and sharp.

Step by Step Instructions

The easiest way to learn Pazurgo® is to simply give it a try. After solving just a puzzle or two, you will discover how intuitive Pazurgo® is, and you will develop your own tricks and techniques for solving the puzzles. Similar to the pre-solved word provided in each puzzle ("HAWAII" in the example shown), the object is to solve each of the Trivia clues by finding the solution word in the puzzle by forming a "chain" linking the letters of the word together. Similar to Hangman, the number of blanks next to each clue indicates the length of each solution word.

1. Beginning with the pre-circled and highlighted starting letters (the circled H's in this example), each letter of the solution word chain is discovered in turn in a horizontal or a vertical direction from the previous letter (there are no diagonal solutions). A line is drawn linking two consecutive letters in a word, crossing out any letters of the puzzle which fall in between.

1. Home to Waikiki H A W A I I
2. Made famous by Nathan's (2 words) _ _ _ _ _ _
3. Large African water-loving mammal _ _ _ _ _ _
Scramble: Smaller than a mountain _ _ _ _ _

2. Similar to crossword puzzles, solutions may consist of more than one word. On the easier puzzles (less than 2 stars), the solutions which consist of more than one word are noted, similar to this example. Looking at the example shown, solving the second clue results in the 2 word solution "HOT DOG".

3. Each letter may only be used once for a single solution word, and any letters which are circled may not then be crossed out by a solution word chain. Looking in the example puzzle for "HOT DOG" identifies the Invalid Solution shown, because the starting letter "H" may not be crossed out.

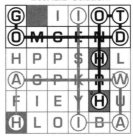

INVALID Solution:

1. Home to Waikiki H A W A I I
2. Made famous by Nathan's (2 words) H O T D O G
3. Large African water-loving mammal _ _ _ _ _
Scramble: Smaller than a mountain _ _ _ _

4. Any letters which are crossed out may no longer be used in a solution word. Looking in the example puzzle for "HOT DOG" identifies the Invalid Solution shown, because the letter "G" which is circled has already been crossed out, and may not be part of the solution.

INVALID Solution:

1. Home to Waikiki H A W A I I
2. Made famous by Nathan's (2 words) H O T D O G
3. Large African water-loving mammal _ _ _ _ _
Scramble: Smaller than a mountain _ _ _ _

5. A solution word chain may cross over itself, or cross over the chain of another solution, but a chain may not cross through the black squares. The only correct solution for "HOT DOG" is shown.

1. Home to Waikiki H A W A I I
2. Made famous by Nathan's (2 words) H O T D O G
3. Large African water-loving mammal _ _ _ _ _
Scramble: Smaller than a mountain _ _ _ _

6. When all of the Solution words have been discovered, the remaining letters which are not circled or crossed out will form the solution to the "Scramble" clue, when those letters are unscrambled in the correct order. In the example, the indicated letters "I", "H", "L", and "L" are the letters which make up the Scramble solution, "HILL".

Just give the patent pending puzzles a try, and I'm sure you will love Pazurgo®! Visit us online at www.Pazurgo.com.

1. Home to Waikiki H A W A I I
2. Made famous by Nathan's (2 words) H O T D O G
3. Large African water-loving mammal H I P P O
Scramble: Smaller than a mountain H I L L

H	G	L	K	O	B	E	S		H	C	B	P	U	A
K		O	M	Z	S	J	N	B	B	F	F	A	C	V
S	G	W	B		Q	U	E	E	J	A	E	S	L	L
I	I	C	O	E	Q	G	Q		R	I	E	Q	E	B
N	G	E	R	V	A	U	Q	S	P	Z	M	O	J	K
A	T	O	D	S	A	C		I	N	T	Y	Z	P	A
B	W	N	N	J	M	W	N	P	G	H	E	C	C	R
S	Y	F	U	S	O	C	A	F	M	D	Y	D	B	N
O	U	V	L	C	M	M	Y	S	M	U	G	B	U	A
Q	T	R	B	C	I	I	S	G	K	R	W	D	F	R
U	A	G	G		N	F	G		H		N	K	I	H
M	H	O	X	A	C	W	S	I	E	G	X	T	L	L
N	W	T	W	L	R	Z	X	U	G	E	C	N	V	I
Y	D	R	B	S	N	X	P	I	O	D	L	R	S	K
T	I	P	N		G	S	E	F	L		G	A	G	N

A4000002

1. Run or Drive (2 words) _ _ _ _ _ _ _ _ _ _ _ _ _
2. Even the professional athletes pay their own way _ _ _ _ _ _ _ _
3. Walking on frozen water **S N O W S H O E I N G**
4. Green Thumb _ _ _ _ _ _ _ _ _
5. Watch out for sharks! _ _ _ _ _ _ _ _
6. ERA, BB, K, RBI, AB, HR _ _ _ _ _ _ _ _
7. Make sure to choose the right suit _ _ _ _ _ _
8. S'mores, hot dogs, and RV parks _ _ _ _ _ _ _
9. Where sand meets water _ _ _ _ _ _
10. AKA objectives _ _ _ _ _ _
11. Big and tall players _ _ _ _ _ _ _ _ _ _ _
12. Where men shave their legs _ _ _ _ _ _ _ _ _
13. Spray-on is better for you _ _ _ _ _ _ _ _ _
14. Pelé made the sport known _ _ _ _ _ _ _
15. In a car or on water _ _ _ _ _ _ _
16. Backyard summer ritual _ _ _ _ _ _ _ _ _
Scramble: Indoor or outdoor events _ _ _ _ _ _ _ _ _

Difficulty: ★☆☆☆☆

N	A	I	E	R	■	E	N	G	U	L	U	A	I	L
A	S	G	F	M	L	Z	O	H	O	T	P	G	E	C
H	G	G	W	T	C	J	Y	(S)	X	A	Z	N	R	P
Q	T	O	M	H	C	K	W	(L)	A	■	S	T	X	A
D	O	V	U	R	A	B	I	■	Y	H	O	C	O	W
H	(N)	K	D	I	N	F	I	U	O	L	L	I	F	B
A	P	K	T	R	C	H	(C)	(H)	T	A	B	W	U	■
(S)	G	H	V	P	R	A	H	(L)	■	N	O	V	H	(C)
L	A	E	L	■	D	Z	I	I	T	K	N	B	P	X
E	Y	V	(C)	(J)	(O)	■	E	S	Q	R	Y	Q	A	O
O	W	(L)	(W)	(U)	(N)	(H)	U	R	H	P	Q	E	(C)	O
B	D	S	(O)	Z	(C)	U	X	Z	M	G	D	N	P	E
(S)	E	T	■	(T)	S	E	J	(N)	K	B	Y	B	I	M
S	A	G	O	(N)	E	M	(N)	L	V	V	A	J	H	C
R	Y	E	I	B	S	C	F	K	M	Y	Y	I	R	D

1. Loud sounds _ _ _ _ _
2. Crustaceans great with butter _ _ _ _ _ _ _ _ _ _
3. "Fruit" from palm trees C O C O N U T
4. . . . of Notre Dame _ _ _ _ _ _ _ _ _ _
5. Web making superhero _ _ _ _ _ _ _ _ _ _
6. Elevation of zero (2 words) _ _ _ _ _ _ _ _ _ _
7. Is the best medicine _ _ _ _ _ _ _ _
8. Ten gallon Texas apparel (2 words) _ _ _ _ _ _ _ _ _ _
9. Princess, Opera, Diamond, or Choker, for example _ _ _ _ _ _ _ _ _
10. Hurricane of the Pacific _ _ _ _ _ _ _
11. Ho Ho Ho (2 words) _ _ _ _ _ _ _ _ _ _ _ _
12. Wings beat 90 times a second _ _ _ _ _ _ _ _ _ _ _ _ _
13. A Doctor's partner _ _ _ _ _ _
14. Iguana or gecko _ _ _ _ _ _ _
15. Bismarck's home (2 words) _ _ _ _ _ _ _ _ _ _ _ _
16. Knee high by the Fourth of July (4 words) _ _ _ _ _ _ _ _ _ _ _ _ _
Scramble: Medical treatment center _ _ _ _ _ _ _ _ _

N	W	E	L	L	Ⓕ	M	R	O	F	J	W	S	G	T
T	F	S	R	O	■	E	E	O	D	R	L	P	Y	B
R	V	E	F	Ⓙ	R	Y	O	K	E	J	B	V	S	N
R	Y	G	G	N	J	L	B	A	S	E	Q	A	Ⓕ	O
O	U	E	R	J	H	T	P	S	■	O	M	T	O	Ⓑ
Q	L	S	I	B	■	Ⓑ	W	T	B	Z	F	H	X	A
Ⓕ	■	Ⓕ	P	I	Ⓒ	X	Ⓝ	A	S	F	S	Ⓑ	B	C
L	M	E	D	E	K	K	I	S	H	Z	Ⓙ	C	O	
W	O	X	C	A	L	Q	N	K	M	N	D	M	H	
J	A	B	A	Ⓙ	Ⓔ	Ⓞ	Ⓤ	■	Ⓑ	T	Ⓑ	B	I	■
M	C	S	J	Z	W	T	H	O	I	U	Ⓑ	U	K	S
A	C	Y	A	Ⓕ	O	R	Y	X	O	A	N	L	F	L
U	S	U	H	W	U	X	R	D	■	D	R	A	U	M
U	G	B	G	E	K	Ⓙ	O	Q	Ⓕ	H	B	N	M	V
M	P	T	O	A	C	P	L	R	A	Ⓙ	O	J	R	D

BB000002

1. Up and down motion of the ball **B O U N C E**
2. Won 10 NCAA Championships in 12 years (2 words) _ _ _ _ _ _ _ _ _ _ _ _
3. Quick movement up court (2 words) _ _ _ _ _ _ _ _ _ _ _
4. Mr. Clutch (2 words) _ _ _ _ _ _ _ _ _ _
5. Off the glass (2 words) _ _ _ _ _ _ _ _ _
6. Limited to 5 or 6 _ _ _ _ _ _
7. Rebounding position (2 words) _ _ _ _ _ _ _
8. Releasing while in the air (2 words) _ _ _ _ _ _ _ _ _ _
9. A shot next to the rim (2 words) _ _ _ _ _ _ _ _ _ _ _
10. His Airness _ _ _ _ _ _ _
11. Tough to defend _ _ _ _ _ _ _ _ _
12. Foul shot (2 words) _ _ _ _ _ _ _ _ _ _ _
13. Big Game James (2 words) _ _ _ _ _ _ _ _ _ _ _ _
14. Rodman, Pippen, Paxson _ _ _ _ _ _
15. Comes in small and power _ _ _ _ _ _ _
16. Name of 2004 NBA expansion team _ _ _ _ _ _ _ _
17. Denver's Chris Andersen _ _ _ _ _ _ _
Scramble: Coach who won the 1999 NCAA Championship (2 words) _ _ _ _ _ _ _ _ _ _ _ _

Difficulty: ★☆☆☆☆☆

A	L	H	O	B	H	X	E		I	S		B	L	D
Y	G	H	C	M	U	R	L	S	O	B	N	D	M	V
R	W	T	O	K	N	D	D	E	L	P	D	U	M	O
R	U	A	P	R	K	I	U		A	Z	K	T	E	
E	Q	P	O	B	A	Z	L	V	X	I	F	A	J	D
L	W	P	D	G		U	E	C	X	C	U	E	H	P
I	O	R	S	Z	Q	I	A	E	T	K	T	R	J	E
U	C	A	T	E		C	K	L	O	J	E	R	E	
X		A	V	B	L	N	O	B	P	R	E	A	V	E
M	A	V	G	E	V	F	M	S	E	D	L	C	H	T
U	T	B	S	Z	L	I	Y	C	C	T		A	U	G
R	F	S		A	A	E	E	M	I	M	D	Q	H	I
W	I	H	L	N	K	T	E	D	K	B	O	P	G	N
E	O	O	Y	Q	T	T	J	O	U	I	G	F	C	E
S	A	K	W	K	K	Y	M		S	F	E	N	T	U

G7100039

1. Goes well with spaghetti _ _ _ _ _ _ _ _ _ _

2. Black and White to Flat Screen _ _ _ _ _ _ _ _ _ _ _

3. An Inuit _ _ _ _ _ _ _

4. Sailor shirt wearing Disney character (2 words) _ _ _ _ _ _ _ _ _ _ _ _

5. Have long snouts and tongues for insects _ _ _ _ _ _ _ _ _ _ _

6. Home of the Wolverines _ _ _ _ _ _ _ _ _

7. Krispy Kreme's specialty _ _ _ _ _ _

8. Granny Smith or Red Delicious _ _ _ _ _ _

9. Has nearly replaced the written letter _ _ _ _ _ _

10. A school instructor _ _ _ _ _ _ _

11. Back to back games (2 words) _ _ _ _ _ _ _ _ _ _ _ _ _

12. Holiday of the empty tomb and a bunny E A S T E R

13. King of Camelot _ _ _ _ _ _ _

14. A blessing or heavenly gift _ _ _ _ _ _ _ _

15. Popular Father's Day gifts _ _ _ _ _ _ _ _ _ _ _ _

16. Scrooge McDuck cartoon (2 words) _ _ _ _ _ _ _ _ _ _

Scramble: Slow reptiles _ _ _ _ _ _ _ _

T	C	Y	G	U	H	Q	S	E	G	O	L	H	E	I
O	X	C	S	T	I	N	M	M	T	R	K	L	M	J
P	I	T	V	C	W	P	A	F	X	Y	O	U	X	N
N	W	N	F	E	G	V	Z	L	F	J	T	U	Q	I
T	N	A	E	C	Y	A	N	O	A	C	N	A	S	C
	W	I	M	O	W	G	B	T	O	J	H	V	G	R
R	B	E	E	A	N	A	P	A	M	N	A	R	C	I
W	E	P	E	W	T	S	U	T	J	D	Q	A	I	V
G	T	Y	H	F	I	Q	T	W	D	M	J	U	G	E
B	P	B	L	O	U	N		I	O	N	L	W	L	U
A	X	A	X	R		E	A	R	R	I	S	K	A	I
S	O	E	H	Y	E	U	P	B	W	V	D	D	G	A
C	D	A	C	Z	W	R	D	Q	N	B	K	L	K	G
V	Z	Z	D	E	K	T	P	S	F	L	I	P	T	I
U	I	R	E	G	W	N	I		I	T		N	W	O

LG000002

1. There were thirteen _ _ _ _ _ _ _ _ _
2. The Preamble (3 words) _ _ _ _ _ _ _ _ _ _ _ _ _ _
3. Two and two are four _ _ _ _ _ _ _ _ _ _
4. That small state (2 words) _ _ _ _ _ _ _ _ _ _ _ _
5. Print and cursive **W R I T I N G**
6. Our country's foundation _ _ _ _ _ _ _ _ _ _ _ _ _
7. A treaty is an . . . _ _ _ _ _ _ _ _ _ _ _
8. Father of our country _ _ _ _ _ _ _ _ _ _ _ _
9. Key to finding a circle's area _ _ _ _ _ _ _
10. One of the three R's _ _ _ _ _ _ _ _ _
11. Charles Lindbergh's solo flight _ _ _ _ _ _ _ _ _ _
12. 90 degrees is right _ _ _ _ _ _
13. Home to Bridgeport and New Haven _ _ _ _ _ _ _ _ _ _ _ _
14. America's greatest heartache _ _ _ _ _ _ _ _ _
15. A man of many words _ _ _ _ _ _ _
Scramble: Citizens have these _ _ _ _ _ _ _ _

B	X	H	D	U	F	R	E	S	L	U	O	X	N	E
P	V	W	O	U	T	Y	H	O	Y	F	L	Y	Y	G
C	C	S	E	D	A	K	E	A	C	F	F	D	Y	U
U	T	L	J	L	E	S	I	G	S	B	E	G		F
M	F	P	F	T	H	C	Q		B	O	C	T	U	N
	B	P	Y	S	T	M	X	S	Y	V	M	T	L	N
N	E	H	M	N	R	I	F	O	E	N	H	J	O	
I	J	K	E		E	O	M	B		T	E	O	J	B
F	E	I	Q	T	G	L	I	E	S	G	R	I	F	P
R	C	U	P	P	N	S	L	B	C	T	K	Z	G	U
A	P	S	U	E	R	B	G	U	C	Z	K	O	F	
Q	A	B	Z	O	P	D	A	R	A	M	P	B	W	E
R	G	G	O	U	P	D	N	E	J	W	A	A	T	K
A	C	N	C	P	N	B	I	G	T	G	V	I	V	L
	N	A	O	U	R		E	H	G	A	X	S	H	

G7100040

1. Harlem trotted this _ _ _ _ _
2. Hair to a bird _ _ _ _ _ _ _
3. Caramel and chocolate's partner _ _ _ _ _ _ _ _ _ _ _ _
4. Tiger Woods has mastered using these (2 words) _ _ _ _ _ _ _ _ _ _ _ _
5. They supposedly bury their heads in the sand _ _ _ _ _ _ _ _ _
6. Carved for Halloween _ _ _ _ _ _ _
7. A monkey's favorite food B A N A N A
8. Hitting this part of your arm isn't very humorous _ _ _ _ _ _ _ _ _
9. Bedtime outfits _ _ _ _ _ _ _
10. Orange's large cousin _ _ _ _ _ _ _ _ _ _
11. Romantic or relaxing in the tub (2 words) _ _ _ _ _ _ _ _ _ _ _
12. The air we breathe _ _ _ _ _ _ _
13. Found behind the movie theater concession stand (2 words) _ _ _ _ _ _ _ _ _ _ _ _ _ _
14. Rich chocolate _ _ _ _ _ _
15. A popular target _ _ _ _ _ _ _ _ _
16. They try to obtain 4 stars _ _ _ _ _ _ _ _ _
17. Roasting or baking stoves _ _ _ _ _ _
Scramble: Aerobic or strength training _ _ _ _ _ _ _ _

R	M	A	R	D	N	G	■	Y	T	E	K	S	N	G
P	W	P	W	Q	Y	W	E	E	I	U	C	K	J	N
E	L	M	V	J	Y	I	J	H	Q	U	C	C	I	M
U	W	X	S	N	I	T	T	O	Z	R	M	K	L	U
M	U	C	R	F	F	G	I	■	W	I	C	Q	L	A
B	Y	X	N	P	D	T	X	I	P	D	M	O	H	S
A	L	T	Y	E	B	S	L	J	Z	E	E	R	M	D
N	F	G	M	M	O	T	A	S	H	C	X	F	E	L
I	Q	V	B	H	W	U	O	T	N	V	D	E	H	P
G	R	E	L	H	A	R	H	E	H	H	G	K	A	I
Y	E	N	R	N	W	■	I	N	E	I	W	U	R	S
I	B	D	C	U	L	G	N	I	N	C	I	L	R	E
T	C	Z	N	N	I	R	O	D	O	V	X	R	■	
C	F	A	S	A	S	G	F	O	O	L	L	L	A	T
D	H	E	R	R	D	D	Z	O	■	C	E	N	■	E

A4000026

1. Duties around the house **C H O R E S**
2. Pot scrubbing, towel drying _ _ _ _ _ _ _ _ _ _ _ _
3. Missing due to lack of sleep _ _ _ _ _ _ _
4. A break in the day _ _ _ _ _
5. Bills, APR, points, miles (2 words) _ _ _ _ _ _ _ _ _ _ _ _ _
6. Yard maintenance "fun" (2 words) _ _ _ _ _ _ _ _ _ _ _ _ _
7. This cutout exists for cats, too (2 words) _ _ _ _ _ _ _ _ _
8. Interior Designers do this _ _ _ _ _ _ _ _ _
9. Take your shoes off _ _ _ _ _ _ _ _ _
10. A group of interacting people _ _ _ _ _ _ _ _ _ _
11. The way a person lives _ _ _ _ _ _ _ _ _ _ _
12. Dirty clothes, hamper, ironing _ _ _ _ _ _ _ _
13. Having these change your life forever _ _ _ _ _ _ _ _
14. Having company over _ _ _ _ _ _ _ _ _ _ _ _
15. Goes well with a healthy diet _ _ _ _ _ _ _ _
Scramble: Ring the bell (2 words) _ _ _ _ _ _ _ _ _ _

Difficulty: ★☆☆☆☆

P	T	I	D	N	Ⓦ	B	O	F	U	E	O	U	W	O
N	J	O	B	A	R	L	R	I	L	I	P	Y	D	S
V	H	N	H	Ⓘ	U	U	P	L	D	B	K	L	X	E
E	N	B	O	B	N	F	Ⓚ	W	E	Z	W	J	N	R
D	E	E	R	K	M	F	X	Z	G	Ⓚ	L	G	G	■
Q	A	S	R	V	C	D	F	Y	G	C	F	A	C	R
Ⓘ	Y	Ⓡ	X	U	Y	N	E	Z	Y	H	B	W	Ⓘ	W
B	L	L	E	C	Q	K	■	I	Ⓦ	O	T	O	T	E
E	X	Q	Z	R	K	K	C	N	A	P	E	Ⓦ	A	
W	I	J	T	Ⓚ	S	T	U	E	Ⓦ	T	Ⓚ	B	Ⓘ	
K	■	E	G	J	R	A	L	G	G	H	Ⓡ	U	K	R
A	P	M	C	Ⓘ	W	H	E	I	E	E	D	L	B	E
R	I	V	D	V	I	O	B	R	Ⓚ	S	S	Ⓞ	C	Ⓓ
E	Y	H	Ⓡ	S	U	O	N	Y	A	■	K	Ⓜ	Q	U
D	R	G	P	V	N	■	G	A	A	Ⓚ	I	■	Ⓝ	G

G7100041

1. The Big Bad Wolf's "Hood" (2 words) _ _ _ _ _ _ _ _ _ _ _
2. Famous soccer event (2 words) _ _ _ _ _ _ _ _ _
3. Creative design or gadget _ _ _ _ _ _ _ _ _ _ _
4. A Monarchy, Empire K I N G D O M
5. A straight edge _ _ _ _ _ _
6. Ice houses _ _ _ _ _ _ _
7. Free Willy (2 words) _ _ _ _ _ _ _ _ _ _ _
8. A popular thing to try to lose _ _ _ _ _ _ _
9. Untamed animals _ _ _ _ _ _ _ _ _
10. Ben and Jerry's mastered this (2 words) _ _ _ _ _ _ _ _ _
11. Hopping marsupials _ _ _ _ _ _ _ _ _ _ _
12. An elastic paper holder (2 words) _ _ _ _ _ _ _ _ _ _ _ _
13. Thoughts _ _ _ _ _ _
14. Red seed popular in chili (2 words) _ _ _ _ _ _ _ _ _ _ _
15. The Bluegrass state _ _ _ _ _ _ _ _ _
16. Gossip station at work (2 words) _ _ _ _ _ _ _ _ _ _ _ _
17. Smooched _ _ _ _ _ _
Scramble: Popular seeded berry _ _ _ _ _ _ _ _ _

C	Z	H	O	I	Y	V	C	F	R	P	E	I	V	N
U	H	D	J	F	O	E	T	Q	B	G	I	U	H	A
B	D	I	C	C	X	M	A	L	C		T	S	A	
L	E	S	C		C	E	M	F	B	N	P	B	E	
S	E		T	R	K	N	E	K	C		O	P	X	S
Z	G	C	B	P	A		R	M	B	S	I	E	M	F
Q	O	C	E	G	L	H	C	C	A	R	P	Q	D	T
O	U	L	C	E	I	Y	D	Q	C	S		R	U	O
O	O	O	D	N	T	A	N	X	C	C	I	U	L	O
N	T	B		M	W	P	E	B	M	B	D	B	B	M
N	E	H	R	N	D	U	B	R	T	F	C	B	M	U
W	A	D	A	J	Z	A	F	Y	B	O	D	S	K	C
V	G	S	C	O	I	F	C	J	A	B	H	P	J	A
K	U	S	E	W	V	T	S	M	B	A		R	U	I
H	L	F	R	C	N	S	R	U	M	C	T	B	E	E

BB000004

1. Some are L-shaped _ _ _ _ _
2. Holds water _ _ _ _ _ _ _
3. Cools pies on shelves (2 words) _ _ _ _ _ _ _ _ _ _ _
4. First created in 1837 by Charles Babbage _ _ _ _ _ _ _ _
5. Hanging light fixture _ _ _ _ _ _ _ _ _
6. Hold on to this so you don't fall _ _ _ _ _ _ _ _ _
7. Lets light in or keeps it out _ _ _ _ _ _ _ _
8. Used for storage **C L O S E T**
9. One of four vertical supports _ _ _ _ _ _ _
10. A place for fine magazines and books (2 words) _ _ _ _ _ _ _ _ _ _ _ _ _
11. Skirting and molding _ _ _ _ _ _ _ _ _ _
12. Sweeps stuff away _ _ _ _ _ _
13. Encyclopedias are likely found here _ _ _ _ _ _ _ _ _
14. Window coverings _ _ _ _ _ _ _ _ _
15. Stool, sofa, loveseat _ _ _ _ _ _ _
Scramble: A Glory Box (2 words) _ _ _ _ _ _ _ _ _ _ _

B	C	U	W	O	I	R	D	N	B	U	I	R	J	R
S	R	L	E	Z	H	G	Y	G	T	C	G	L	V	I
E	R	K	F	H	E	F	S	E	O	P	G	G	K	N
D	Y	W	J	S	P	W		N	F	A	A	U	H	E
T	Q	T	L	Y	H	V	C	O	P	O	H	N	O	V
S	B	B	X	A	N	A	H	N	S	B	G	J	A	A
S	E	X	I	B	D	W	G	A	Q	D	G	V	L	C
N	M	M	R	T	Z	Q	W	Y	T	I	H	W	J	A
G	X	W	M	U	W	V	H	C	A		H	Y	U	S
V	U	H	Z	H	T	A	T	H	U	E	P	M	E	
K	N	I	Y	P	N	I	R	F	T	A	V	E	K	S
A	U	L	O	P	G	B	D	W	A	O	O	N	B	U
A	O	D	N	Q	S	E	P	B	P	B	M	C	F	O
I	U	H	W	R	M	A	L	V	O	N	H	K	P	Y
S	C	N	X	W	I	V	A	R	L	B	A		A	C

G7100043

1. Hot magma flows from this _ _ _ _ _ _ _ _
2. Men are from Mars, women are from . . . _ _ _ _ _ _
3. Top cheese producing state _ _ _ _ _ _ _ _ _ _
4. Male fowl known for extravagant tail feathers _ _ _ _ _ _ _ _
5. Home to the city, Lisbon _ _ _ _ _ _ _ _ _
6. A panda's favorite food _ _ _ _ _ _ _
7. A Kansas staple _ _ _ _ _ _
8. Holiday, sabbatical _ _ _ _ _ _ _ _ _ _
9. Known for their metamorphosis B U T T E R F L I E S
10. The Father of the US _ _ _ _ _ _ _ _ _ _ _ _
11. The only bird that can fly backwards _ _ _ _ _ _ _ _ _ _ _ _ _
12. Wrist accessories _ _ _ _ _ _ _ _
13. A dog's favorite spot for a potty break _ _ _ _ _ _ _ _
14. Carnivore native in the Arctic (2 words) _ _ _ _ _ _ _ _ _ _
15. Celebrations for the future birth of a child (2 words) _ _ _ _ _ _ _ _ _ _ _ _ _
16. Also called a cyclone _ _ _ _ _ _ _ _ _ _
Scramble: Contains 51 miles of Lake Erie shoreline _ _ _ _ _ _ _ _ _ _ _ _

R	R	R	O	L		S	R	N	N		R	E	P	N
E	G	H	X	D	L	F	A	A	B	M	V	C	O	E
E	V	H	Q	F	L	O	O	S	J	W	O	E	N	U
Q	E	K	I	Y	K	S	O	C	I		S	E	B	T
E	O	U	F	C	U	Y		L	A	A	E	H	O	
V	C	W	H	P	A	A	Y	T	O	T	D	P	A	C
M	A		U	R	B	D	S	E	T	K	H	J	A	
C	D	M	F	U	N	N	D	S	T	K	I	M	T	S
F	F	N	E	O	Y	I	J	K	G	W	N	C	D	B
E	I	I	E	Z	A	S	T	D	F	O	U	C	B	M
C	G	S	L	E	M	I	F	R	B	W	J	R	C	
A	G	L	R	P	C	Q	R	E	M	I	S	F	Z	O
C	A	D	S	R		D	S	S	Y	G	O	F	E	D
G	R	M	U	S	R	P	P	L	T	W	F	N	Z	C
N	C	I	G	X	A	K	E	H	D	L	X	K	E	A

A4000011

1. On every corner _ _ _ _ _ _ _ _ _ _
2. Needed for those with a bad habit (2 words) _ _ _ _ _ _ _ _ _ _ _ _ _ _
3. Comes in lumps _ _ _ _ _
4. For the lactose intolerant (2 words) _ _ _ _ _ _ _ _
5. A necessity in a car (2 words) _ _ _ _ _ _ _ _ _ _
6. A "hot" alternative to coffee _ _ _ _ _ _ _ _ _ _ _ _
7. Coffee doesn't percolate by itself! (2 words) **C O F F E E M A K E R**
8. Sugar substitutes _ _ _ _ _ _ _ _ _ _ _
9. Non-fat milk _ _ _ _ _ _ _
10. A powder or liquid _ _ _ _ _ _ _ _
11. It takes a lot to maintain a coffee habit _ _ _ _ _ _ _ _
12. Leaded vs. unleaded _ _ _ _ _ _ _ _ _
13. Ordered by those who want just a regular cup of Joe (2 words) _ _ _ _ _ _ _ _ _ _ _
14. Coffee's partners after dinner _ _ _ _ _ _ _ _ _
15. Hot enough to burn _ _ _ _ _ _ _ _ _
16. A good latte topper _ _ _ _ _ _ _ _ _
Scramble: Smoother and more sugary (2 words) _ _ _ _ _ _ _ _ _

T	Z	A	R	F	D	K	C	N	B	E	B	T	R	S
W	O	D	O	B	W	K	G	H	M	U	R		U	
E	E	W	S	G	Q	O	I	R	C	W	C	E	Y	T
S	O	F	F	U	D	T		A	D	O	Y	G	E	C
O	Z	X	X	K	U	V	C	N	A	S	F	F	I	N
R	H	D	C	P	W	H	E	R	S		E	V	H	A
A	T	R	D	O	X	V	Q	O	O	N	X	M	U	L
N	J	C	B	V	I	I	M	R	C	R	R	C	J	O
N	I	T	C	O	M	A		S	I	E	M	S	E	C
B		J	L	G	Q	I	E	S	C	S	P	S	A	R
G	R	U	A	X	E	U	T	I	Z	H	Q	A	P	P
L	K	E	M	N	M		M	B	E	P	N	L	C	
S	E	U	Y	C		T	I	I	O	Z	G	F	Y	M
I	Y	B	X	G	Q	Z	R	E	C	A	I	B	H	A
C	L	O	E	P	C	U	V	E	T	J	I	N	J	Y

A4000001

1. Needs to follow the leader _ _ _ _ _ _ _ _ _ _ _ _
2. No stamps needed _ _ _ _ _ _
3. Suits, sports box and jets _ _ _ _ _ _ _ _ _ _ _
4. Too many of these can get you fired _ _ _ _ _ _ _
5. The drive to and from work _ _ _ _ _ _ _ _
6. Sometimes done by "tele" _ _ _ _ _ _ _ _ _ _
7. They're bossy _ _ _ _ _ _ _ _ _
8. Given with the benefit of the doubt _ _ _ _ _ _ _ _
9. Purpose, goals, and a statement _ _ _ _ _ _ _ _
10. Lunch time activity _ _ _ _ _ _ _ _ _ _ _ _ _
11. Used to "close the deal" _ _ _ _ _ _ _ _ _ _ _
12. Workplace prison cells _ _ _ _ _ _ _ _ _
13. High level pay _ _ _ _ _ _ _ _ _ _
14. Quality and Integrity, for example **C O R E V A L U E S**
15. The name on employee paychecks _ _ _ _ _ _ _
Scramble: The coming together of communications _ _ _ _ _ _ _ _ _

Difficulty: ★☆☆☆☆

L	G	L	I	J	A	E	L	I	P	U	O	T	E	J
E	J	H	O	H	L	J	P	S	S	E	V	Z	K	E
S	K	A	B	T	M	Y	L	J	H	F	M	P	R	L
T	N	J	C	N	E	I	■	W	G	T	N	B	T	■
C	B	Y	C	O	Q	E	N	D	N	U	I	T	I	A
S	V	V	U	P	D	U	A	K	R	■	E	A	R	O
Y	E	K	A	N	P	P	J	X	H	L	Y	R	U	Z
F	N	■	I	W	D	T	S	Q	A	B	P	■	K	C
G	I	A	Z	R	■	G	A	C	A	U	J	R	Y	L
A	O	P	F	R	K	X	M	I	Z	B	I	S	D	F
L	N	L	M	N	E	E	B	M	E	O	T	■	I	L
H	X	S	A	C	T	E	J	L	N	A	I	D	D	O
I	P	M	Q	■	I	Y	M	B	N	H	N	W	Y	C
I	J	J	S	T	S	C	S	A	U	A	C	G	B	S
O	J	N	L	R	P	R	■	M	U	R	R	N	N	G

G7100036

1. A thunderstorm's output _ _ _ _ _ _ _ _ _
2. From an oyster _ _ _ _ _ _
3. Went up the hill (3 words) _ _ _ _ _ _ _ _ _ _ _ _ _
4. Usually monogamous between a couple _ _ _ _ _ _ _ _ _ _ _ _ _ _
5. Green with . . . _ _ _ _ _ _ _ _ _
6. Kermit, or Dunham's Peanut, for example **P U P P E T**
7. Weekday evening TV (2 words) _ _ _ _ _ _ _ _ _ _
8. Baby Kangaroos _ _ _ _ _ _
9. Old TV-top antennas (2 words) _ _ _ _ _ _ _ _ _ _ _ _
10. Small kidney-shaped candy treat (2 words) _ _ _ _ _ _ _ _ _ _ _
11. Wedding ring alternative to gold _ _ _ _ _ _ _ _ _
12. A twisted doughy ballpark staple _ _ _ _ _ _ _ _
13. Christmas-time red and green plant _ _ _ _ _ _ _ _ _ _ _ _
14. Raggedy Ann or Andy (2 words) _ _ _ _ _ _ _ _
15. Popular on the front porch (2 words) _ _ _ _ _ _ _ _ _ _ _
Scramble: A crossroads _ _ _ _ _ _ _ _ _

C	E	Y	S	S	J	I	P	F	R	C	Q	U	N	O
U	J	R	T	M	V	H	V	E	O	N	N	D	K	K
X	L	K	V	T	A	P	F	E	W	N	U	M	S	K
X	A	I	W	P	M	Z	P	L	P	P	K	B	T	I
L	U	B	C	C	L	A	I	G	W	T	X	S	L	A
T	S	G	J	H	M	E		O	C	H	J	O	I	D
T	I	X	E	G	C	P	D	C	C	C	B	O	T	Z
Y	I	E	O	W	D	R	B	R	B	Q	K	E	K	U
R	G	G	V	U	T	T	E	G	E	C	T		J	Z
W	P		K	C	M	F	N	P	I	R	E	I	R	A
T	Q	P	T	E	Q	L	P	I	C	R	M	P	I	N
A	O	A	O	V	N	P	G	T	V	V	L	K	M	G
L	Y	U	U	K	A	C	C	X	Z	H	A	H	M	L
I	U	Y	N	Z	R	E	C	F	F	Q	A	L	W	A
T	I	W	B	C	O	P	T	T	T	L	R		N	N

LG000001

1. A farmer's weed problem _ _ _ _ _ _ _ _ _
2. More than one bovine _ _ _ _ _ _ _
3. When things go well the farm is . . . _ _ _ _ _ _ _ _ _ _ _ _
4. A rancher's pride and joy _ _ _ _ _ _ _ _
5. When a rancher's a midwife _ _ _ _ _ _ _ _ _ _ _ _ _ _
6. See them rolling along _ _ _ _ _ _ _ _ _ _ _
7. Just a tilling up the land _ _ _ _ _ _ _ _ _
8. A cow's lawn _ _ _ _ _ _ _ _
9. Grain bins are filled to . . . **C A P A C I T Y**
10. Required to figure out all the future work _ _ _ _ _ _ _ _ _
11. Passed from one generation to the next _ _ _ _ _ _ _ _ _ _ _ _
12. A farmer's work is never done _ _ _ _ _ _ _
13. I think I will saddle up old . . . _ _ _ _ _ _
14. A helpful Chevy or Ford _ _ _ _ _ _ _ _ _ _ _ _
Scramble: Hybrid of wheat and rye _ _ _ _ _ _ _ _ _ _

Difficulty: ★☆☆☆☆

```
N E A E R ■ C I Ⓓ Ⓝ Y P A X T
A D W U M M J P Ⓣ Ⓩ Ⓡ H U Ⓐ H
G H D V N Y S L Ⓢ Z C D O Ⓟ Y
Y C I Q B O N X Ⓢ Ⓐ ■ E T Y C
E R O U A I D F ■ R E A E H I
F Ⓞ G D I C L G C W J B Z A P
J D U N J O R Ⓞ Ⓐ K C M V D ■
Ⓢ M L B P G S I R ■ V I U B Ⓢ
A K A S ■ Ⓞ ■ S E G Q N Q O Q
N V S L Z A R O Ⓐ Z A X U D H
K M Ⓞ W T N P M P C V X R Ⓢ T
L V A T F Ⓐ Q T A P O Ⓐ A G S
Ⓐ R H O A O J E R R W I U C Y
A S I A Ⓢ N L X B W W K U Y E
M M O T F I M P F Ⓞ R J T E R
```

G7100037

1. Home of the Falcons, Hawks, and Braves _ _ _ _ _ _ _ _
2. Site of Arrivals and Destinations _ _ _ _ _ _ _ _
3. A top amateur athlete _ _ _ _ _ _ _ _
4. Needed for wrapping presents (2 words) _ _ _ _ _ _ _ _ _ _ _
5. Reached by dialing zero _ _ _ _ _ _ _ _ _
6. A bunker on a golf course **S A N D T R A P**
7. Popular fruity baby food _ _ _ _ _ _ _ _ _ _
8. Paint between eggshell and semi-gloss _ _ _ _ _ _
9. Musical instrument for polkas _ _ _ _ _ _ _ _ _ _
10. Partners with a razor (2 words) _ _ _ _ _ _ _ _ _ _ _ _ _
11. Home of the Razorbacks _ _ _ _ _ _ _ _ _
12. Tulsa's home _ _ _ _ _ _ _ _ _
13. Web making superhero _ _ _ _ _ _ _ _ _
14. The Swiss Family Robinson and Robinson Crusoe's ordeal _ _ _ _ _ _ _ _ _ _ _
15. Tropicana (2 words) _ _ _ _ _ _ _ _ _ _ _
16. Shrek and Fiona _ _ _ _ _ _
Scramble: Looking at the stars _ _ _ _ _ _ _ _ _

T	T	I	C	M	D	B	S	R	U	E	D	D	L	O
D	Z	F	Z	P	A	R	E	A	F	M	I	T		P
A	V	X	V	O	P	X	O	N	G	W	G	U	T	F
U	W	R	S	C	E	X	S	N	Q	S	O	A	J	C
J	W	H	N	H	R	Z	S		A	R	R	K	Q	I
H	S	I	J	I	O	V	F	E	Z	R	T		S	P
O	V	T	A	G	H	B	R	F	G	N	T	C	A	
O	W	N		X	A	L	A	S	T	E	K	J	Z	R
I	H	J	G	Q	T	K	M	A	R	A	A	L	R	A
E	K	T	R	H	E	E	M	V	K	K	R	Q	T	P
T	C	I		A	L		G	E	T	U	W	D	S	T
A	A	N	A	N	E	Y	C	N		N	Q	D	D	P
E	F	E	D	U	V	T	I	A	Y	E	M	U	O	T
I	M	R	R	P	E	C	M	A	T	I	D	J	A	T
B	L	P	U	T		O	V	K	I	L	A	A	G	N

G7000014

1. A leisure traveler _ _ _ _ _ _ _ _
2. A permanent move _ _ _ _ _ _ _ _ _ _ _
3. Required for boarding _ _ _ _ _ _ _
4. Used to fly the friendly skies _ _ _ _ _ _ _ _ _
5. Meals for a lazy traveler _ _ _ _ _ _ _ _ _ _ _ _ _
6. A game or hobby _ _ _ _ _ _ _ _ _
7. Site for fine dining _ _ _ _ _ _ _ _ _ _ _
8. Hailed on a street corner _ _ _ _ _ _ _
9. The goal of a beach vacation _ _ _ _ _ _ _ _ _ _ _
10. The land down under _ _ _ _ _ _ _ _ _
11. Provides service in the skies _ _ _ _ _ _ _ _ _ _
12. Online or In person booking assistant T R A V E L A G E N C Y
13. An exciting undertaking _ _ _ _ _ _ _ _ _
14. Journeys for business or pleasure _ _ _ _ _ _
15. A travel companion from Hertz _ _ _ _ _ _ _ _ _
Scramble: In foreign lands _ _ _ _ _ _ _

Difficulty: ★☆☆☆☆

A	J	L	L	N	P	X	A	E	T	P	L	E	O	R
L	E	U	M	G	E	F	Y	K	Y	K	Q	U	R	M
O	T	A	M	G	G	H	R	Y	E	M	L	T	L	A
U	V	Q	L	E	A	W	Z	K		B	F	L	L	E
D	R	V	A	T	Q	X	T	I		E	U		E	C
A	G	L	U	J	W	R	C	U	I	J	O	X	W	T
F	P	E	G	N	U	P	X	Q	H	E	P	G	L	E
Q	I	R	E	H	K	C	T	R	J	R	Z	O	P	A
I	N	S	G	K	O	P	R	K	L	K	Y	P	Z	E
Q	E	Q	A	R	V	I	I	E	A	T	A	R	F	Q
L	P	Q	Y	G	E	G	B	I	U	I	P	K	V	T
R	R	B	M	M	N	O	W	L	Q	K	E	E	L	T
O	W	A	S	E	S	H	R	O	E	I	O	W	O	D
S	H	S	O	E	O	Z	M	I	Q	V	N	J	A	G
E	Y	L	D	S	L	T	R	L	T	E		R	O	E

G7100048

1. A big shake _ _ _ _ _
2. When children vault over each other's backs _ _ _ _ _ _ _ _ _
3. Small rodent often kept as a pet _ _ _ _ _ _ _
4. Halloween requirement for candy (3 words) _ _ _ _ _ _ _ _ _ _ _ _ _ _
5. Subtropical sour citrus fruit _ _ _ _ _ _ _ _ _ _
6. A necessity in bathrooms (2 words) _ _ _ _ _ _ _ _ _ _ _ _ _ _
7. Person licensed to practice law _ _ _ _ _ _ _
8. Punctuation used for noting a spoken phrase _ _ _ _ _
9. Shushed _ _ _ _ _ _ _
10. English or Spanish, for example _ _ _ _ _ _ _ _ _
11. Stage between childhood and adulthood _ _ _ _ _ _ _ _ _ _
12. These types of houses are edible _ _ _ _ _ _ _ _ _ _ _ _ _
13. Person who prevents drownings _ _ _ _ _ _ _ _ _
14. Canadian province with French as the official language _ _ _ _ _ _ _
15. The pyramids were built from this L I M E S T O N E
16. Measured in degrees _ _ _ _ _ _ _ _ _ _ _
Scramble: Largest of the primates _ _ _ _ _ _ _ _

L	Ⓡ	L	E	S	■	R	U	A	T	A	N	O	W	I
E	X	J	H	S	T	F	E	I	Y	L	X	G	E	T
N	R	O	G	O	A	K	M	Ⓘ	P	M	R	I	R	J
■	Y	T	B	S	I	C	J	Ⓡ	E	■	S	T	Q	A
U	Z	V	N	F	S	U	D	Ⓤ	Ⓒ	O	D	Ⓣ	Ⓐ	
W	N	I	L	M	N	J	O	Ⓑ	Ⓑ	R	F	M	Ⓡ	
Q	O	B	L	Q	Y	M	Ⓐ	Ⓢ	Ⓢ	Ⓚ	L	V	H	R
T	Ⓘ	N	K	G	C	A	G	R	■	R	I	K	H	Ⓐ
U	O	I	C	D	Ⓐ	W	O	D	A	G	C	U	X	Y
S	F	T	R	T	■	R	E	Ⓘ	V	E	X	O	M	M
N	P	Ⓘ	Y	E	T	S	P	N	N	Z	Q	I	Ⓢ	K
T	Z	E	H	T	Ⓢ	C	T	S	F	F	Ⓢ	M	C	U
Ⓐ	C	R	A	P	U	L	M	A	U	Z	H	E	N	G
T	N	W	I	R	Q	T	H	B	W	V	B	K	M	R
E	M	N	N	C	G	■	E	F	Ⓡ	L	M	E	T	R

A4000007

1. Grammy's, Dove, AMA's, etc. _ _ _ _ _
2. Popular site to download music _ _ _ _ _ _
3. Usually done "digitally" for old songs _ _ _ _ _ _ _ _
4. Classical music group _ _ _ _ _ _ _ _ _ _ _
5. The random function _ _ _ _ _ _ _
6. Someone trying to become professional _ _ _ _ _ _ _
7. At least one is needed to make music _ _ _ _ _ _ _ _ _ _
8. The traditional source for music purchases _ _ _ _ _ _ _ _ _
9. Sounds like popular artists _ _ _ _ _ _ _ _ _ _
10. Offers a free download each week <u>S</u> <u>T</u> <u>A</u> <u>R</u> <u>B</u> <u>U</u> <u>C</u> <u>K</u> <u>S</u>
11. A type of music and guitar _ _ _ _ _ _ _ _
12. A classic "satisfying" group _ _ _ _ _ _ _ _ _ _ _ _
13. Millions of people vote and watch each week _ _ _ _ _ _ _ _ _ _ _ _ _
14. A large record label _ _ _ _ _ _ _ _ _
15. The newer place to purchase music _ _ _ _ _ _ _ _
Scramble: American music started in the 40's and 50's _ _ _ _ _ _ _ _ _ _ _

R	X	V	H	I	Ⓐ	E	Ⓐ	O	Q	B	N	R	W	O
C	T	T	U	M	G	A	U	F	L	D	V	J	F	W
O	G	H	I	K	F	G	A	U	Ⓒ	P	A	M	S	
I	Y	G	U	T	O	F	M	E	M	O	S		D	L
E	S	R	L	Y	L	C	N		Ⓐ	B	Z	V	I	Y
G	Ⓒ	C	H	R	Ⓔ	Ⓑ		Ⓔ	Ⓔ	U	I	I	J	I
P	Y	L	H	A	Ⓣ	D	Q	W	N	Ⓑ	R	E	N	G
M	V	Ⓒ	R	T	L		I	P	D	A	F	N	L	A
N	B	W	H	I	R	A	K	Ⓒ	Z	W	O	I	J	W
H	T	R	N	S	F	C	S	D	D	L	N	S	X	T
	O	D	J	O	T	L	Y	T	E	A	Z	B	Q	R
R	F	V	P	I	S	O	T	Ⓐ		E	K	Ⓑ	K	
H	Ⓑ	O	U	C	U	D	Q	O	C	R	V	A	X	L
X	L	Z	W	I	O	J	M	N	Ⓐ	T	B	S	E	B
E	G	T	Y	S	I	T	I	C	S	U	Ⓐ	U	A	I

G7100001

1. Opening this causes more trouble than it's worth _ _ _ _ _ _ _ _ _ _ _
2. In the space which separates **B E T W E E N**
3. Experts or leaders _ _ _ _ _ _ _ _ _ _ _ _
4. Qualities of sound in an auditorium _ _ _ _ _ _ _ _ _ _ _
5. New shoes may cause this _ _ _ _ _ _ _
6. Down under _ _ _ _ _ _ _ _ _
7. Gaining the affection of; dating _ _ _ _ _ _ _ _ _
8. Appeal, lure _ _ _ _ _ _ _ _ _ _
9. Jack's adventure _ _ _ _ _ _ _ _ _ _
10. A house, church, or skyscraper _ _ _ _ _ _ _ _
11. Unwilling, reluctant _ _ _ _ _ _ _
12. Freshwater "lobster" _ _ _ _ _ _ _ _ _
13. To think about carefully _ _ _ _ _ _ _ _
14. A coalition _ _ _ _ _ _ _ _ _
Scramble: Refinement _ _ _ _ _ _ _

M	E	P	F	I	P	U	Y	T	A	E	N	O	N	V
G	T	O	J	V	N	E	L	B	R	O	V		V	L
A	W	L		A	H	W	J	H	M	W	A	R	I	C
E	F	B	H	O		E	R	S	E	K		A	M	P
S	L	O	T	S	Y	U	U	W	M	Z	A	N	A	U
D	B	N	S	H	C	I	O	L	Y	J	J	O	F	E
A	J	R	Z	H	B	K	N	O	G	K	R		R	D
J	L	K	K	C	A	B	O		H	G	T	N	A	N
J	R	H	Q	Z	R	D	E	L	G	M	M	N	O	C
B	U	J	D	O	Q	U	L	I	H	W	U	T	X	A
	G	E	G	O	I	A	C	L	A	M	E	M	Q	I
K	P	A	I	M	D	E	E	N	L	R	X	B	V	J
X	E	X	S	I	U	K	J	W	Z	O	Y	B	U	
T	N	J	M	J	I		T	D	W	R	C	I	M	E
T	N	G	F	Y	Q	F	O		A	R	R	J	S	O

BB000006

1. The Iron Horse _ _ _ _ _ _ _ _ _ _
2. Passed 700 home runs _ _ _ _ _ _
3. Legendary Miami QB _ _ _ _ _ _ _
4. Broadway Joe _ _ _ _ _ _ _ _ _
5. Magic's Rival _ _ _ _ _ _ _ _ _ _
6. Boxer Sugar Ray _ _ _ _ _ _ _ _
7. The Bambino _ _ _ _ _ _ _ _ _
8. The Catch _ _ _ _ _ _ _ _ _ _ _
9. Female athlete stripped of 5 gold medals _ _ _ _ _
10. Coached "Da Bears" _ _ _ _ _ _ _ _ _ _ _
11. Led NFL in rushing in 8 of his 9 seasons _ _ _ _ _ _ _ _ _
12. Coached Jordan **J A C K S O N**
13. Big Game James _ _ _ _ _ _ _ _ _ _ _ _ _
14. The Fight of the Century, 1971 _ _ _ _ _ _ _ _ _ _ _ _ _ _
15. Round Mound of Rebound _ _ _ _ _ _ _ _
16. The Mailman _ _ _ _ _ _ _
Scramble: The Merry Mex _ _ _ _ _ _ _ _ _ _

E	T	A	L	I	B	L	L	R	E	H	U	M	L	A
R	G	G	X	A	O	G	H	E	R	B	C	X	O	I
■	I	I	L	K	I	F	C	V	F	F	M	O	F	■
E	P	O	Q	T	A	W	L	H	J	■	R	Y	O	O
R	E	U	D	Y	O	U	A	T	N	B	G	I	A	V
E	F	I	L	S	F	T	K	N	A	J	G	R	T	I
F	Y	I	E	Q	R	I	M	I	A	K	S	W	C	S
B	E	S	I	Q	A	U	M	I	E	B	R	N	S	I
N	R	W	R	O	X	G	N	N	M	P	M	Z	L	A
H	E	F	E	■	L	F	F	J	F	T	L	O	■	Z
I	O	O	N	D	N	R	E	■	R	R	D	V	C	P
D	H	W	Q	K	R	V	X	E	A	Y	L	L	C	A
M	R	F	W	V	I	F	E	U	T	M	F	Z	B	S
Y	H	C	J	N	Z	A	N	L	N	N	S	P	T	A
I	A	A	L	R	P	E	Z	■	S	E	■	S	O	R

1. Pink tropical birds _ _ _ _ _ _ _ _ _ _
2. A shortstop or first baseman _ _ _ _ _ _ _ _ _ _
3. A sponsored show found around 3am _ _ _ _ _ _ _ _ _ _ _ _ _
4. The best players of a professional sport _ _ _ _ _ _ _ _ _
5. A hit which isn't fair _ _ _ _ _ _ _ _ _
6. Closely personal _ _ _ _ _ _ _ _
7. Unable to read _ _ _ _ _ _ _ _ _ _
8. A kind act or service _ _ _ _ _ _
9. Criminals taken into custody _ _ _ _ _ _ _
10. Scared, terrified _ _ _ _ _ _
11. The London Eye or Texas Star _ _ _ _ _ _ _ _ _ _ _ _ _
12. A helpful act or sports play A S S I S T
13. The Emerald Isle _ _ _ _ _ _ _
14. A home for ice cream _ _ _ _ _ _ _
15. Winner of seven majors _ _ _ _ _ _ _ _ _ _ _
Scramble: Travel account _ _ _ _ _ _ _ _ _

G7100002

D	S	■	B	O	I	T	N	L	P	■	L	E	C	I
R	K	M	P	A	L	H	A	A	H	Y	K	J	E	H
R	V	C	Y	E	O	G	O	W	Y	I	Q	N	R	G
W	E	D	F	P	E	R	C	C	D	T	D	D	F	S
B	I	W	K	P	D	L	Y	■	S	P	R	U	W	A
M	W	M	H	S	P	X	C	U	E	X	F	C	R	Z
L	A	A	E	G	H	O	C	C	S	J	J	L	E	M
D	I	T	K	A	F	O	B	R	■	X	I	W	W	U
R	U	O	Z	R	D	O	S	S	Y	C	T	W	W	U
E	Z	T	H	E	H	K	C	S	P	J	R	H	E	Q
R	B	V	K	E	L	F	X	A	U	M	E	G	J	T
M	L	C	N	T	S	W	I	T	R	O	S	B	N	Y
A	B	C	W	Q	G	Q	P	S	N	C	U	E	L	V
H	B	C	E	E	N	E	A	Z	V	A	G	B	P	T
■	U	T	R	U	I	D	I	C	D	O	V	F	T	A

A4000005

1. Protection from rocks, bugs and rain _ _ _ _ _ _ _ _ _ _ _
2. Required attire in any car _ _ _ _ _ _ _ _ _ _ _
3. These are sometimes missing from Jeeps _ _ _ _ _ _
4. The heart of the engine cooling system _ _ _ _ _ _ _ _ _ _
5. A bad name or a way to check the "level" _ _ _ _ _ _ _ _ _ _
6. To keep the rain at bay _ _ _ _ _ _ _ _ _ _ _
7. It's usually better to let the car manufacturer add this option _ _ _ _ _ _ _
8. A left leg workout so you don't grind _ _ _ _ _ _ _
9. A necessity so your car doesn't overheat _ _ _ _ _ _ _
10. Locking your doors is a form of this _ _ _ _ _ _ _ _ _
11. There are never enough of these in a car _ _ _ _ _ _ _ _
12. Rarely needed anymore with "injected" cars **C A R B U R E T O R**
13. Missing for a car up on blocks _ _ _ _ _ _ _
14. Predecessor to the mp3 player _ _ _ _ _ _ _ _ _
15. A home for Bobble heads, hula girls, etc. _ _ _ _ _ _ _ _ _ _
16. The Club was a popular attachment for this _ _ _ _ _ _ _ _ _ _ _ _ _
Scramble: Operates under the car _ _ _ _ _ _ _ _ _ _

O	D	O	M	Z	U	A	R	U	■	K	A	U	F	L
R	P	P	E	D	N	J	V	A	■	F	Q	G	Z	E
Ⓡ	C	J	R	B	B	Ⓒ	C	C	E	C	T	Ⓡ	E	E
E	H	H	I	M	I	■	T	Q	E	M	L	K	O	L
■	P	N	E	E	Z	Ⓒ	M	Ⓒ	R	S	Ⓡ	Y	X	O
B	P	P	U	R	H	H	E	B	Ⓡ	R	R	A	A	L
L	I	■	P	E	E	C	■	W	W	P	K	M	U	Ⓒ
T	S	V	O	X	H	B	L	W	E	P	Ⓒ	A	I	E
X	A	O	K	Ⓒ	E	J	L	A	N	F	X	C	V	G
E	■	Ⓡ	U	I	U	A	J	V	L	E	N	E	U	A
R	Q	S	A	F	T	R	G	E	A	C	T	■	Y	W
■	O	Ⓒ	■	Ⓝ	M	Ⓔ	Ⓓ	O	T	Ⓡ	C	I	H	N
I	B	V	D	Ⓘ	B	Ⓖ	Ⓞ	Z	Z	O	D	M	T	■
G	P	A	I	Y	Z	G	Ⓖ	K	P	E	F	I	L	R
S	N	Ⓡ	E	Q	Y	R	Ⓒ	R	S	D	N	A	T	E

G7100004

1. Cruise ship of the Mississippi _ _ _ _ _ _ _ _ _
2. Birds of prey _ _ _ _ _ _ _ _
3. Invented an expression C O I N E D
4. Saint Nick's steeds _ _ _ _ _ _ _ _
5. Muscle spasm _ _ _ _ _
6. Contrition for past sins _ _ _ _ _ _ _ _ _ _
7. A tricky pitch _ _ _ _ _ _ _ _
8. Courting or wooing _ _ _ _ _ _ _ _
9. Made a loud rattling sound _ _ _ _ _ _ _ _ _
10. Commonly seen at rinks in the Disco era _ _ _ _ _ _ _ _ _ _ _ _
11. Mats for your drink _ _ _ _ _ _ _ _ _
12. To think carefully about _ _ _ _ _ _ _ _ _
13. Site of Prague _ _ _ _ _ _ _ _ _ _ _ _ _
14. Someone who flees to safety _ _ _ _ _ _ _ _
15. Men's 2000 Olympics soccer champion _ _ _ _ _ _ _ _
Scramble: Divulge _ _ _ _ _ _

P	X	A		R	L	O	C	H	R	B	E	T	S	C
M	I	U	D	H	I	H	X	R	A	R	W	I	H	L
L	I	P	K	J	Y	A	I	Y	X	F	C	H	O	E
R	Q	F	D	Q	E	Q	S	F	B	S	P	X	A	N
N	I	T	K	I	B	V	O	O	E	M	H		L	S
Y	F	X	A	S	H	U	H	I	T	I	W	S	P	A
S	E	F	N	T	P	P	L	W	Q	G	V		J	H
S	P	E	P	M	Z	I	K	I	Y	R	J	U	I	N
V	Z	I	J	T	A	S	R	O	A	L	A	X	H	D
V	O	R	E	M	R	E	L	M	E	G	T	C	G	V
E	S	T	S	U	B	Z	G	A	S	N	K	I	K	U
N	K	O	M	J	A	E	I	C	H	H	O	K	L
A	L	U	V	R	N	B	Q	G	T	O	W	U	P	U
A	B	O	D	E	Z	Z	J	R	O	S	V	F	Q	E
T	G	I	O	M	R	R		C	I	S	E	S	I	N

A4000017

1. Athletic events _ _ _ _ _ _ _ _ _ _ _ _ _
2. Your "family" by marriage _ _ _ _ _ _ _
3. A bad environment _ _ _ _ _ _ _ _
4. Not to be avoided _ _ _ _ _ _ _ _ _ _ _
5. Dinner or lunch _ _ _ _ _ _ _
6. Time for just the couple _ _ _ _ _ _ _ _ _
7. The "season" for family time _ _ _ _ _ _ _ _ _
8. Outdoor activities with the family _ _ _ _ _ _ _ _ _ _ _ _ _
9. An adversary or sibling _ _ _ _ _ _
10. A state of well-being and contentment _ _ _ _ _ _ _ _ _ _
11. The basic residential unit _ _ _ _ _ _ _ _ _ _ _
12. Safety, comfort _ _ _ _ _ _ _ _ _
13. Restless or short of temper _ _ _ _ _ _ _ _ _
14. Practice for music, dance, and theater R E H E A R S A L S
15. The main "job" for children _ _ _ _ _ _ _ _ _ _
Scramble: Risk transfer _ _ _ _ _ _ _ _ _

Difficulty: ★★☆☆☆

S	M	H	U	X	V	O	L	N	G	R	D	R	E	T
I	B	O	N	F		T	E	F	E	C	E	W		B
A	N	E	C	S	T	F	F	U	Z	X	D	E	E	T
R	B	F	N	F	D	D	V	M	W	P	M	A	R	G
E	J	L	V	U	R	V	S	K	V	I	O	G	A	I
T	X	H	P	A	E	A	V	I	Q	T	O		H	
F	K	N	C	F	N	S	J	L	G	M	D	F	F	V
A	K	B	E	D	G		W	V	H	V	E	D	W	H
E	J	P	W	A	C	E	A	I	A	R	V	I	V	Q
F	S	H	R	A	Z	G	A	U	C	T	Y	C	N	I
E	Z	N	N	U	P	P	Q	I	U	C	T	F	I	
I	U	L	Q	L	H	Z	N	C	I	K	T	M	F	A
V	Y	F	O	E	X	S	V	J	A	O	A	Y	B	B
I	R	Y	F	F	O	I	C	S	M	S	L	F	M	N
N	I	R	Y	E	N	F	A	I	V	K	O	E	R	

G7100015

1. Pong or Asteroids, for example _ _ _ _ _ _ _ _ _ _ _
2. Granted under the Bill of Rights _ _ _ _ _ _ _ _ _ _ _ _
3. A community _ _ _ _ _ _ _ _
4. Aquatic animals _ _ _ _ _ _ _
5. Teasing, courting _ _ _ _ _ _ _ _ _ _
6. Conclude, close _ _ _ _ _ _ _
7. Each showed heroism on 9/11 _ _ _ _ _ _ _ _
8. Oil and vinegar dressing _ _ _ _ _ _ _ _ _ _ _ _
9. A pepper or squash _ _ _ _ _ _ _ _
10. The London Eye or Texas Star _ _ _ _ _ _ _ _ _ _ _
11. Creates or starts, as in an organization F O U N D S
12. Etna or Mauna Loa _ _ _ _ _ _ _ _
13. Key German city _ _ _ _ _ _ _ _ _ _
14. Home to the Holy See _ _ _ _ _ _ _ _ _ _ _ _
Scramble: Large Falls _ _ _ _ _ _ _ _ _

G	N	V	J	R	K	B	V	E	W	W	T	L	C	E
B		N	I	Y	D	H	I	R	M	Y	M	K	X	M
I	U	A	G	W	Y	G	C	N	W	U	A	O	N	
T	P	P	D	E	Y	P	Q	S	V	K	B	R	M	A
T	E		N	R	I	A	R	K	K	R	A	A	V
I	M	A	U	L	E	V		S	O	A	K	O	H	L
L	W	R	Y	H	N	D	C	I	N	K	O	B	T	A
K	Z	Q	E	P		V	R	V	I	G	K	E	L	B
R	X	R	O	A	B	E	Z	W	K	J	I	R	W	X
H	C	E	V	E	B	D	K	D	U	L	T	C	A
M	S	W	E		E	M	F		C	L	Q	O	M	E
J	E	H	O	E	W	O	B	A	A	E	J	V	E	I
E	P	S	Z	A	A	U	O	S	W	F	W	R	C	U
N	G	A	G	T	T	G	P	U	A	I	F	W		G
G	P	W	I		S	K	I	N	L	E	K	I	T	I

G7000013

1. A side dish to the main course _ _ _ _ _ _ _ _ _ _
2. A soy sauce partner for sushi _ _ _ _ _ _ _
3. Named after New Zealand's flightless bird _ _ _ _ _ _ _ _ _ _
4. Found in a Waldorf Salad _ _ _ _ _ _ _ _
5. A popular French dressing _ _ _ _ _ _ _ _ _ _ _ _
6. Skewered meat dish from the Mediterranean **K A B O B S**
7. A very liquid fruit _ _ _ _ _ _ _ _ _ _ _
8. Cheesy Italian dish of breaded and fried delicate meat _ _ _ _ _ _ _ _ _ _ _ _ _ _
9. One of Uncle Ben's dishes _ _ _ _ _ _ _ _
10. Meat from hunted game _ _ _ _ _ _ _
11. Meat from massaged Japanese cattle _ _ _ _ _ _ _ _ _
12. A black table olive, usually preserved in vinegar or olive oil _ _ _ _ _ _ _ _ _
13. Delicious target of the "Deadliest Catch" _ _ _ _ _ _ _ _ _
14. Harvested grain _ _ _ _ _ _
15. A sweet dessert from southern Florida _ _ _ _ _ _ _ _ _ _ _
Scramble: A key acidic ingredient in European and Asian cuisine _ _ _ _ _ _ _ _ _

Difficulty: ★★☆☆☆

N	D	T	I	B	B	R	C	Q	H	A	X	P	E	N
A	M	Z	A	C	B	B	E	E	I	I	U	M	I	F
T	T	O	V	N	T	O	G	C	H	M	H	O	O	R
U	E	C	G	U	Z	I	P	R	W	U	F	I	B	S
N	V	O	O	O	A	G	Z	X	H	N	P	S	Y	O
A	G	M	D	S	R	Q		M	X	O	S	V	H	L
B	H	M	V	R	K	N	R	L	K	M	U	Z	G	O
T	D	I	P	W	E	T	Y	E	H	Y	J	T	K	Q
	A	C	C	N	L	D	I	C	A	C	C		P	C
T	B	C	P	F	J	K	N	C	I	O	L	O	Z	Z
Y	D	R	Z	Q	K	E	W	T	X	W	A	O	R	R
P	J	C	K	I	E		E	N	T	Y	N	N	C	D
U	D	O	I	C	J	O	C	C	E	C	O	C	T	C
K	Z	F	A	C	O	F	S	E	O	S	L	J	F	O
E	R	R	U	A	I	L	S	V	Z	S	I	A	L	E

G7100017

1. A tool using animal _ _ _ _ _ _ _ _ _ _ _
2. McNaught and Hale-Bopp _ _ _ _ _ _ _
3. Manny Ramirez or Matt Holliday, for example _ _ _ _ _ _ _ _ _ _ _ _
4. Extra-virgin _ _ _ _ _ _ _ _
5. Surgical procedure _ _ _ _ _ _ _ _ _ _ _
6. Ruthless, murderous _ _ _ _ _ _ _ _ _ _
7. O-town or Hollywood East _ _ _ _ _ _ _ _
8. Popular brand of caramel corn _ _ _ _ _ _ _ _ _ _ _ _ _
9. Seat for a chorus member _ _ _ _ _ _ _ _ _ _ _
10. Beginning or cause _ _ _ _ _ _ _
11. Mecca for the NFL C A N T O N
12. An airline and a tire company _ _ _ _ _ _ _ _ _ _ _ _
13. The Godfather of Heavy Metal _ _ _ _ _ _ _ _ _ _ _ _ _
Scramble: The Hunter's sash _ _ _ _ _ _ _ _ _ _ _

T	A	O	O	ⓈS	P	H	S	S	S	R	G	B	R	■
T	V	G	W	B	E	T	H	R	D	T	S	K	F	U
I	M	N	U	Y	V	I	W	ⓈS	E	T	Y	J	I	C
R	K	ⓈS	G	L	O	ⓈS	R	K	O	K	H	ⒻF	F	L
U	O	ⒻF	O	B	E	M	U	N	T	D	■	G	E	N
ⒻF	B	S	■	T	X	Q	G	O	■	K	ⒻF	L	F	R
E	A	B	O	F	H	N	J	R	ⒻF	F	I	N	A	F
■	G	V	W	S	J	E	M	L	U	I	ⓈS	Z	O	
Y	A	D	R	G	A	K	E	■	W	F	X	C	O	B
Y	G	R	P	Z	U	A	Z	P	J	L	I	K	Z	L
R	V	ⒻF	S	U	E	ⓏZ	W	E	G	■	L	X	Q	I
I	C	G	U	Q	I	W	ⓇR	E	Q	ⓈS	E	W	M	ⓈS
ⒻF	H	F	P	L	H	ⒺE	ⒹD	ⓇR	O	N	■	O	A	N
S	M	V	O	O	O	Y	O	O	A	E	I	D	C	D
A	M	F	E	F	D	N	ⒻF	N	ⓈS	L	S	G	N	I

G7OOOOO3

1. A blizzard _ _ _ _ _ _ _ _ _
2. The body's natural reaction to the cold _ _ _ _ _ _ _
3. For high powered rides over snow and ice _ _ _ _ _ _ _ _ _ _ _ _
4. An activity for neighboring snow-covered hills _ _ _ _ _ _ _ _ _ _
5. A winter in the home F R E E Z E R
6. The annual way to avoid influenza _ _ _ _ _ _ _ _
7. A time for presidents, lovers, and the cold _ _ _ _ _ _ _ _ _
8. No two are alike _ _ _ _ _ _ _ _ _
9. Periods of light snow and little accumulation _ _ _ _ _ _ _ _ _
10. The condition when clouds touch the earth _ _ _ _ _
11. Fun for the slopes _ _ _ _ _ _
12. Extreme cold _ _ _ _ _ _ _
13. Machines used to clear driveways _ _ _ _ _ _ _ _ _ _ _ _
14. An unwelcome period of declining health _ _ _ _ _ _ _ _ _
15. Elegant gliding over ice _ _ _ _ _ _ _ _
16. A lake in the winter _ _ _ _ _ _ _
Scramble: Contains Winter as the final concerto _ _ _ _ _ _ _ _ _ _ _

Difficulty: ★★☆☆☆

P	M	N	H	V	D	B	P	U	S	L	C	D	R	
O	Q	E	E	T	W	W	E	G	M	E	V	F	I	K
I	L	R	U	G	L	G	D	L	A	U	J	K	S	L
	A	V	A	R	N	V	B	I	T	H	I	O	N	A
R	E	E	W	A	U	P	T	F	X	K	G	E		R
I	J	N	H	O	G	V	W	K	B	F	I	Y	W	Z
O	H	L	M	I	Z	N	Q	V	Y	J	N	K	N	E
V	V	L	T	N	I	L	S	I	T	W	N	X	L	E
E	L	J	E		R	A	K	U	I	R	H	P	I	L
O	W	O	T	T	E	C	F	I	B	T	O	N	V	I
E	C	K	C	N		D	V	H	M	W	E	Y	V	E
R	W	M	H	O	I	L	A	S	O	H	E	Z	I	R
V	C	B	O	A	K	A	C	Y	N	E			G	M	E
V	T	S	C	W	K	C	C	E	E	L	X	Y	K	P
U	Q	Q	O		T	M	W	R	L	I			S	D	A

G7100058

1. MS Operating System after XP _ _ _ _ _ _
2. Favorable perches for frogs _ _ _ _ _ _ _ _ _
3. City shared by Missouri and Kansas _ _ _ _ _ _ _ _ _ _ _ _
4. 2010 Winter Olympics site _ _ _ _ _ _ _ _ _
5. X-Men Superhero Logan _ _ _ _ _ _ _ _ _
6. A note usually burnt after a breakup _ _ _ _ _ _ _ _ _ _ _ _
7. A time for laundry _ _ _ _ _ _ _ _
8. Generous, compassionate, thoughtful _ _ _ _ _ _ _ _ _ _ _ _ _
9. Firefly _ _ _ _ _ _ _ _ _ _ _ _
10. Caused by motion, as in Energy _ _ _ _ _ _ _
11. Freak, oddball **W E I R D O**
12. A sucker for blood _ _ _ _ _ _ _ _
13. Miss Piggy's beau _ _ _ _ _ _ _
14. A Valentine's gift favorite _ _ _ _ _ _ _ _ _
15. Manitoba capital _ _ _ _ _ _ _ _ _
16. Thin covering over another surface _ _ _ _ _ _ _
Scramble: A popular summer fruit _ _ _ _ _ _ _ _ _ _

Difficulty: ★★☆☆☆

E	Z	Y	I	B	S	T	B	D	B	G	N	T	I	S
M	G	O	Q	R	Z	M	O	C	W	N	U	W	H	A
I	F	G	L	C	B	B	B	A	S	G	A	L	E	I
A	A	F	D	O	P	K	W	S	D	M	K	■	O	L
R	D	T	I	Q	A	A	O	■	S	Q	M	H	O	Z
S	S	S	K	C	I	B	■	C	L	A	B	F	V	L
J	S	P	Y	I	C	B	V	Y	E	B	R	A	N	S
J	L	R	O	S	■	N	F	J	I	R	M	F	R	A
E	O	P	N	X	S	M	Y	S	C	J	T	D	I	D
Y	A	E	N	U	U	I	R	Y	Y	U	A	B	H	O
N	D	E	I	B	I	G	T	■	S	V	Z	F	I	H
C	U	G	S	G	B	W	Z	E	■	U	B	S	D	■
P	K	V	E	X	R	X	K	E	B	H	U	B	H	A
O	S	F	Q	A	E	Z	X	K	L	C	W	A	■	D
R	W	E	T	S	S	E	N	A	R	B	E	L	L	

G7000002

1. For holding lunch, snacks, and drinks _ _ _ _ _ _
2. Speedo, for one _ _ _ _ _ _ _ _
3. A great way to avoid a burn _ _ _ _ _ _ _ _ _ _
4. Inflatable fun for the beach _ _ _ _ _ _ _ _ _ _
5. Much gentler than a gale _ _ _ _ _ _
6. Used to ride the waves _ _ _ _ _ _ _ _ _
7. Can be peddled on a mountain, or on the road _ _ _ _ _ _ _
8. They are a fear of the swimmer and surfer _ _ _ _ _ _
9. Includes a mast, hull, and a keel _ _ _ _ _ _ _ _
10. For wave-riding lying down **B O O G I E B O A R D**
11. When a bucket, shovel, and the beach meet _ _ _ _ _ _ _ _ _ _
12. A five legged ocean wanderer _ _ _ _ _ _ _ _
13. To keep the sand at bay, or fighting the evening chill _ _ _ _ _ _ _ _
14. An unfortunate way to "feed the fishes" on rough seas _ _ _ _ _ _ _ _ _ _ _ _
15. Hot air flying machines _ _ _ _ _ _ _ _
Scramble: A swimmer with wings and stings _ _ _ _ _ _ _ _

E	Y	J	C	C	U	P	F	S	T	V	N	I	N	G
M	I	K	T	O	N	B	S	A	U	M	D	K	U	S
W	Y	U	T	U	U	K	F	E	L	V	V	S	U	M
L	X	G	S	C	F	Z	I	F	E	V	R	M	Z	C
C	Q	I	U	V	D	R	C	O	Z	C	W	G	I	
Q	N	R	P	Q	A	E	B	N	B	I	E	L	F	I
O	Y	H	M	I	N	O	M	M		Y	H	I	K	C
	E	J	W	Y	M	H	N	G	A	N	C	H	M	A
A	C	Y	C	U	O	O		L	E	M	N	R	E	F
N	T	O	Y	P	X	D	G	W	A	F	C	E	T	R
T	A	Z	R	F	M	I	N	M	K	T	F	E	H	E
	I	D	F	N	M	N	E	C	N	C	I	L	O	V
L	L	R	G	F	T	A	T	E	M	X	B	I	F	L
E	J	E	O	J	K	U	P	M	U	P	Q	R	L	K
W	I	P	T	X	I	V	E	D	F	E	N	R	Y	A

A4000004

1. They show these when mad _ _ _ _ _ _ _ _ _ _ _ _
2. Known as this because of their favorite drink _ _ _ _ _ _ _ _ _ _ _ _
3. People are called this a lot when frightened _ _ _ _ _ _ _ _ _ _ _
4. Another name for a cat _ _ _ _ _ _ _
5. Temperamental _ _ _ _ _ _
6. Long or short hair _ _ _ _ _
7. Always there to welcome their owners home _ _ _ _ _ _ _ _ _ _ _
8. Driven by treats _ _ _ _ _ _ _ _ _ _
9. Instigators of trouble **M A S T E R M I N D S**
10. It's great that cats do this to themselves! _ _ _ _ _ _ _ _ _
11. Sly _ _ _ _ _ _ _ _
12. Their independent spirit _ _ _ _ _ _ _ _ _
13. Cleaning with their paws, a cat becomes this after eating _ _ _ _ _ _ _ _ _ _ _
14. They cause destruction to this _ _ _ _ _ _ _ _ _ _ _
15. Their language _ _ _ _ _ _ _ _
Scramble: Pensive _ _ _ _ _ _ _ _ _ _ _ _ _ _ _ _ _

Difficulty: ★★☆☆☆

T	M	E	I	Z	Q	L	P	J	A	I	W	R	S	D
U	U	G	U	C	■	A	R	O	A	F	E	G	A	B
N	O	S	J	T	O	C	W	V	A	B	S	C	E	L
I	A	P	E	K	U	N	M	U	F	V	S	E	I	H
E	B	L	W	H	I	Y	E	Q	Z	J	R	Y	D	S
R	U	J	A	B	E	C	C	W	M	U	A	R	U	G
P	C	X	W	C	P	T	C	W	M	G	N	S	K	W
H	Y	O	A	X	T	N	W	P	W	L	P	I	P	K
■	E	X	R	■	I	L	T	M	T	T	Q	C	Q	P
O	B	V	U	C	F	P	C	F	I	R	H	■	N	I
P	X	S	Z	M	Q	E	P	N	V	F	C	P	O	L
P	G	C	S	O	D	■	L	U	N	K	C	V	Y	E
R	K	Z	A	P	W	C	P	Y	B	B	I	G	J	■
L	Z	G	U	L	A	A	X	O	C	W	U	O	G	R
E	N	H	H	A	R	D	L	B	M	H	P	R	H	T

G7100026

1. A ship's window _ _ _ _ _ _ _ _ _
2. An alligator's cousins _ _ _ _ _ _ _ _ _ _ _ _
3. Most attractive _ _ _ _ _ _ _
4. Decorative designs _ _ _ _ _ _ _ _ _
5. A customer _ _ _ _ _ _ _
6. Geppetto's son P I N O C C H I O
7. contenders, Dark Horses _ _ _ _ _ _ _ _ _ _ _ _
8. The safari's swimming pool _ _ _ _ _ _ _ _ _ _
9. Kitchen cabinet _ _ _ _ _ _ _ _ _
10. An outdoor meal with family _ _ _ _ _ _ _ _ _ _ _ _
11. A photo _ _ _ _ _ _ _ _
12. Beds for children _ _ _ _ _ _
13. Types include computer, tape, and earth _ _ _ _ _ _
14. Front windows for cars _ _ _ _ _ _ _ _ _ _ _ _
Scramble: A Cowboy _ _ _ _ _ _ _ _ _

I	B	W	U	L	P	E	P	A	U	Z	N	A	J	L
O	S	I	O	U	K	Y	A	C	K	H	Y	G	Q	O
K	P	N	A	V	B	V	S	R	P	R	I	D	A	I
E	F	D	K	L	P	C	M	█	E	D	J	Q	N	S
R	S	█	E	O	L	R	U	S	M	V	M	E	T	X
K	E	N	O	S	E	S	█	O	O	N	Y	W	P	A
R	J	T	O	X	A	B	G	F	D	D	Y	R	E	█
S	F	M	N	E	T	E	E	Q	P	D	H	D	P	P
C	B	H	V	T	O	P	K	S	K	U	P	U	W	L
O	W	U	Z	S	I	R	A	G	C	R	Y	Q	F	J
R	D	P	G	█	S	Y	E	U	V	Q	U	B	S	Z
G	L	L	J	A	S	O	L	L	E	H	H	F	Y	L
U	T	I	U	Y	H	Y	T	E	P	N	G	B	A	U
E	I	S	X	A	I	P	G	F	A	Z	I	T	D	S
C	I	B	N	E	C	P	S	I	C	I	V	U	X	C

A4000024

1. Totally, dude! <u>S</u> <u>U</u> <u>R</u> <u>F</u> <u>S</u> <u>U</u> <u>P</u>
2. A dolphin _ _ _ _ _ _ _ _
3. Eaten cooked or raw _ _ _ _ _ _ _ _
4. Enjoyment _ _ _ _ _ _ _ _
5. Usually colder than the Atlantic _ _ _ _ _ _ _ _
6. Found on the beach _ _ _ _ _ _ _
7. Under the sea _ _ _ _ _ _ _ _ _ _ _ _
8. A Spanish "beach" _ _ _ _ _ _
9. Peaceful and free of storms _ _ _ _ _ _
10. Popular dinner attraction _ _ _ _ _ _ _ _ _ _ _ _ _
11. Bring on the Coco Lopez! _ _ _ _ _ _ _ _ _ _ _
12. On top of the sea _ _ _ _ _ _ _ _ _ _ _
13. Better than rocky _ _ _ _ _ _
14. Drinks to take the pain away _ _ _ _ _ _ _ _ _ _ _ _
15. Calmly, quietly _ _ _ _ _ _ _ _ _ _
Scramble: Is an aesthetic ideal _ _ _ _ _ _ _ _ _ _ _ _

D	L	B	B	Ⓕ	E	W	I	E	■	N	H	T	P	H
O	K	S	G	T	T	K	S	Q	R	J	M	E	■	Y
E	Z	P	Ⓢ	F	J	F	M	W	Ⓕ	R	O	N	B	C
A	O	P	■	O	J	M	P	F	Ⓢ	D	L	K	W	A
E	H	V	O	Q	U	R	A	K	C	L	A	W	■	X
T	R	O	Ⓕ	Ⓢ	O	O	D	G	F	C	O	F	W	V
O	R	I	■	O	X	B	T	S	O	L	■	I	D	A
Q	B	Q	A	K	U	T	■	I	G	S	W	E	L	Ⓕ
Ⓢ	M	Z	D	Z	J	H	G	R	A	R	A	V	V	E
■	K	G	E	O	K	R	N	Y	Y	K	H	E	S	■
Ⓕ	J	A	R	B	T	P	L	Ⓓ	Ⓓ	L	Ⓢ	H	Ⓕ	I
A	G	L	U	U	I	G	L	V	Q	F	H	P	N	S
F	Z	X	Ⓢ	C	Ⓝ	F	C	C	Ⓔ	Ⓕ	R	V	C	V
O	Z	E	O	F	X	I	A	Y	S	R	F	F	X	Y
T	Y	■	N	■	Ⓛ	Ⓨ	■	Ⓤ	M	Ⓢ	L	E	L	E

G7100005

1. Le Parisien brass instrument _ _ _ _ _ _ _ _ _ _ _ _
2. When a movie failed or bombed _ _ _ _ _ _ _ _
3. A ledge _ _ _ _ _ _
4. Color changing, late afternoon opening flowers _ _ _ _ _ _ _ _ _ _ _ _ _
5. The human body _ _ _ _ _ _
6. Desert insect with pincers and a poisonous sting _ _ _ _ _ _ _ _ _
7. Used for heating and cooking _ _ _ _ _ _
8. The London Eye and Texas Star _ _ _ _ _ _ _ _ _ _ _ _ _ _
9. Occurring unexpectedly <u>S</u> <u>U</u> <u>D</u> <u>D</u> <u>E</u> <u>N</u> <u>L</u> <u>Y</u>
10. Key German city _ _ _ _ _ _ _ _ _
11. The medium for Aesop and the Brothers Grimm _ _ _ _ _ _ _ _ _ _
12. Site of the Black Hills _ _ _ _ _ _ _ _ _ _ _ _
13. Home to Bratislava _ _ _ _ _ _ _ _ _
14. The best locations on baseball bats for a hit _ _ _ _ _ _ _ _ _ _ _ _
Scramble: Delicate _ _ _ _ _ _ _ _

H	D	Y	A	X	X	I	J	L	S	X	E	V	M	R
S	F	B	M	H	U	P	E	I	S	V	F	V	H	E
P	N	U	J	D	P	D	O	U	M		C	I	E	
L	E		S	C	P	S	V	E	S	X	M	Z	A	R
S	H	N		S	M	A	P	E	S	S	N	Z	T	G
O	O	A	C	X	O	A	R	N	Q	O	P	T	T	J
C	R	O	I	W	T	R	G	P	I	M	I	L	V	S
K	P	U	K	E	I	A	R	U	A	Y		O	N	Y
L	N	C	R	O	A	I	U	N	F	Q	X	W	U	A
	C	W	U	E	J	S	E	M	Q	N	R	L	L	L
S	W	P	N	V	G	S	V	U	T	F	C	S	T	A
C	B	A	I	B	B	I	G	Z	M	S	Z	Y	E	F
S	F	K	P	R	O	H	D	H	I	L	H	L	D	O
C	L	R	R	L	K	U	C	B	G	I		S	Q	O
S	T		E	C	U	S	E	A	G	C	Y	G	T	O

A4000008

1. Two sides coming to an agreement _ _ _ _ _ _ _ _ _ _ _
2. Fees which decrease the longer you own your car _ _ _ _ _ _ _ _ _ _ _
3. Commission, plaid pants, stereotypes _ _ _ _ _ _ _ _ _ _ _ _ _
4. Funding alternative to financing _ _ _ _ _ _ _ _
5. A common characteristic in sales _ _ _ _ _ _
6. Repeat buyer characteristic _ _ _ _ _ _
7. Airbags, seatbelts, etc. _ _ _ _ _ _ _
8. This class costs more than the economical one _ _ _ _ _ _
9. Corvette, Ferrari, Porsche, etc. **S P O R T S C A R**
10. You can be this way with so many car options _ _ _ _ _ _ _
11. Every car needs these to maintain its operation _ _ _ _ _ _ _ _ _
12. Common way to pay for cars _ _ _ _ _ _
13. Hesitant when buying a used car _ _ _ _ _ _ _ _ _
14. A common feeling from sales when car shopping _ _ _ _ _ _ _ _
15. Personal factors which determine the car purchase _ _ _ _ _ _ _ _ _ _ _ _
Scramble: A necessity to earn returning clients _ _ _ _ _ _ _ _ _ _ _ _ _

Difficulty: ★★⯪☆☆

F	E	O	O	H	Q	O	S	P	E	U	H	R	I	**F**
L	U	**N**	F	F	**K**	**S**	■	A	N	L	T	M	F	F
R	Q	**A**	E	E	W	H	**F**	L	O	B	**P**	R	X	E
■	M	**P**	D	P	R	D	E	■	C	C	Q	T	S	E
N	Y	R	E	L	C	Y	N	N	G	Q	L	E	C	E
W	U	A	A	O	O	U	R	J	K	N	E	H	W	O
A	U	I	B	X	**D**	D	I	I	A	S	**D**	S	T	L
Y	I	S	R	R	E	A	■	L	V	P	E	■	D	E
K	■	I	T	H	T	D	E	F	F	I	**P**	T	E	T
D	L	U	K	O	B	N	**P**	S	A	D	R	C	J	H
■	O	P	H	G	C	O	X	G	I	R	■	M	V	O
R	J	E	■	**F**	I	N	A	A	**F**	N	P	I	P	**D**
P	G	W	E	U	C	R	**D**	C	Z	I	Y	T	C	R
U	P	G	T	T	■	H	E	G	L	M	A	F	R
■	D	Z	T	V	W	D	O	■	A	I	R	**F**	W	A

G7100012

1. Diminished, weakened _ _ _ _ _ _ _ _
2. The Nature Isle of the Caribbean _ _ _ _ _ _ _ _
3. The medium for Aesop and the Brothers Grimm _ _ _ _ _ _ _ _ _ _ _
4. Very improbable _ _ _ _ _ _ _ _ _ _
5. Popular white and yellow flowers _ _ _ _ _ _ _ _
6. Household appointments _ _ _ _ _ _ _ _ _
7. Grassland burrowing rodents _ _ _ _ _ _ _ _ _ _ _ _
8. Negligent, overdue _ _ _ _ _ _ _ _ _ _ _
9. Site for halftime "divot stamping" _ _ _ _ _ _ _ _ _ _
10. An Enzo or F40 _ _ _ _ _ _ _ _
11. America's first European settlement _ _ _ _ _ _ _ _ _ _
12. The London Eye and Texas Star _ _ _ _ _ _ _ _ _ _ _ _
13. Hot dogs **F R A N K S**
14. Large shrimp _ _ _ _ _ _
15. Chrysler's Ram _ _ _ _ _ _
Scramble: An executive course _ _ _ _ _ _ _ _

H	O	S	E	T	H	E	E	F	R	U	M	B	T
E	K	N	O	N	T	M	R	T	U	A	M	M	L	S
L	W	E	J	C	A	Z	L	M	P	X	N	U	J	R
L	P	E	Y	L	N	F	C	B	U	G	N	B	C	E
O	L	P	H	B	V	W	C	C	Y	C	N	D	O	
C	I	O	P	B	N	I	C	P	Q	E	C	W	C	M
F		T	H	E	R	L	A	C	L	F	A	M	D	B
E	L	E	Y	T	Q	G	O	O	C	A	F	S	P	E
M	D	Z	K	I	A	U	D	R	O	U	T	T	A	
P	I	G	K	F		E	N		T	T	F	K	O	D
P	S	D	Z	P	R	E	R	L	X	E	C	L	G	K
E	Y	R	A	D	A	W	S	B	A	I	A	O	V	C
F	H	A	L	I	E	U	F	Q	N	R	X	R	V	E
I	S	W	U	M	K	B	Y	H	I		M	S	D	D
S	I	C	E	K	T	A	J	C		C	H		L	D

A4000003

1. Contains a pad of paper and pen _ _ _ _ _ _
2. It usually has wheels _ _ _ _ _ _
3. Math for dummies! _ _ _ _ _ _ _ _ _ _ _
4. A morning staple in many break rooms _ _ _ _ _ _ _
5. Most of us stare at one all day _ _ _ _ _ _ _ _ _
6. Used for filing _ _ _ _ _ _ _ _
7. They retract on their own _ _ _ _ _ _ _ _ _ _ _ _
8. A communication device in your pocket _ _ _ _ _ _ _ _ _ _
9. It's either too slow or too fast most days _ _ _ _ _
10. A now ancient way of sending docs _ _ _ _ _ _ _ _ _ _
11. Manila _ _ _ _ _ _ _ _
12. You can swallow one or write on one _ _ _ _ _ _ _
13. Still often preferred over sending emails _ _ _ _ _ _ _ _ _ _ _
14. Usually only one can be open at a time _ _ _ _ _ _ _ _ _ _ _ _
15. To set timelines and meetings _ _ _ _ _ _ _ _
16. A helpful item to increase time management _ _ _ _ _ _ _ _
17. Found in an airport or at your desk T E R M I N A L
Scramble: In a monitor or in your office _ _ _ _ _ _ _ _

Difficulty: ★★⯪☆☆

L	H	K	Z	J	Z	P	A	A	F	N	O	D	G	E
X	R	C	G	R	A	V	B	C	A	A	S	■	V	C
I	H	L	D	Z	Y	Z	A	L	C	P	H	S	O	I
B	W	H	V	T	C	C	A	E	U	P	K	R	A	U
U	L	B	I	Q	U	E	J	P	M	E	T	U	E	R
J	E	L	T	P	E	S	U	A	U	S	E	K	Y	I
N	H	X	I	A	D	■	V	U	■	F	W		T	S
■	Y	N	Q	K	J	N	N	M	L	E	B	U	Q	Z
H	Y	R	A	U	O	U	■	N	C	■	L	N	A	U
P	I	G	T	Z	F	N	A	J	R	E	N	S	W	T
M	B	M	U	V	C	S	T	W	O	F	B	D	I	R
E	R	N	A	G	C	U	U	U	V	O	X	A	Q	O
S	G	V	W	E	S	S	I	U	L	P	Q	A	C	R
N	M	E	X	K	K	R	X	E	■	L	M	S	X	M
I	N	E	P	F	A	N	O	N	C	P	O	B	T	O

G7100013

1. Site of the Masters _ _ _ _ _ _ _ _
2. Referee _ _ _ _ _ _ _
3. Hay fever reactions _ _ _ _ _ _ _ _ _ _ _
4. Development, enlargement _ _ _ _ _ _ _ _ _ _ _
5. New York's capital _ _ _ _ _ _ _
6. Former USSR site of Tashkent _ _ _ _ _ _ _ _ _ _ _
7. Seven emirates _ _ _ _ _ _ _ _ _ _ _ _ _
8. Furious, irate _ _ _ _ _ _
9. Twilights _ _ _ _ _ _ _ _
10. Personification of the US _ _ _ _ _ _ _ _ _
11. Strength of electrical current A M P E R A G E
12. A boa _ _ _ _ _ _ _ _ _ _ _ _ _
13. Polynesian island with large statues _ _ _ _ _ _ _ _ _ _ _ _ _
14. The smallest country in Central America _ _ _ _ _ _ _ _ _ _ _
15. A French nobleman _ _ _ _ _ _
Scramble: Usual home to the "19th hole" _ _ _ _ _ _ _ _ _ _

D	A	M	A	N	V	Q	O	A	W	A	X	C	L	I
C	C	X	R	Z	R	A	S	T	C	V	N	R		C
E	H	N	P	E	U	U	U	E	Y	H	I	H	R	Y
R	X	M	G	E	S	U	Q	A	G	P	I	O	J	F
B	X	G	V	P	N	U	T	O	R	C	U	Q	T	B
Y	D	U	R	R	R	I	P	L	V	C	D	A	I	A
E	Z	B	R	B	Q	K	B	Z	M	C	D	A	D	R
S	D	L	S	C		A	N	E	A	C	O	J	N	O
	N	A	I	D	N	Y	K	B	A	W	B	D	D	Y
I	T	D	Y	A	J	S	W	O	C	O	G	V	C	L
N	S	E	M	Z	A	A	L	U	C	U	P	H	J	A
L	E		D	B	F	S	A	C	E	G	X	Z	G	N
D	T	O	Q	T	R	R	O		O	S	B	M	B	
L	F	I	J	C	Z	O	K	C	D	K	T	G	A	N
L	S	S	U	R	A		N	H	A	I	R	O	B	E

BB000007

1. Indoor ski slope _ _ _ _ _
2. Capital of Argentina _ _ _ _ _ _ _ _ _ _ _ _
3. Northwest FL, premier beach destination _ _ _ _ _ _ _
4. Rio de Janeiro, Sao Paulo, Amazon _ _ _ _ _ _
5. Coronado, Lake Tahoe, Yosemite _ _ _ _ _ _ _ _ _ _
6. Copenhagen, Valdemar Palace _ _ _ _ _ _ _
7. Grand, known for diving _ _ _ _ _ _ _ _ _ _ _ _ _ _
8. Southern tip of Baja, Mexico _ _ _ _ _ _ _ _ _ _ _ _
9. St. George's Town, Hamilton, coral reefs _ _ _ _ _ _ _
10. Aspen, Mile-High City _ _ _ _ _ _ _ _
11. Mt. Coot-tha, Queensland _ _ _ _ _ _ _ _
12. West of Tampa, Caladesi Island, Pinellas County _ _ _ _ _ _ _ _ _ _ _
13. German home to many Japanese companies _ _ _ _ _ _ _ _ _ _
14. US island, famous red-roofed hotel _ _ _ _ _ _ _ _
15. Chinese home to the world's largest shopping mall **D O N G G U A N**
Scramble: Site of The Arc de Triomphe _ _ _ _ _ _ _ _ _

Difficulty: ★★⯪☆☆

A	P	U	D	A	L	E	■	N	O	E	J	R	T	Y
C	K	G	G	K	G	G	A	■	I	F	D	F	D	T
R	A	M	Y	V	H	N	S	E	V	S	Ⓡ	Ⓡ	I	K
E	B	X	B	N	O	B	M	N	K	D	U	Z	G	C
B	M	Ⓖ	Y	N	G	E	■	A	L	V	H	G	B	
Y	C	S	I	J	B	L	S	E	Q	Ⓡ	D	E	L	I
R	Ⓖ	G	E	T	F	A	Ⓡ	P	K	Ⓡ	O	M	I	E
R	E	A	O	Ⓡ	R	B	R	L	I	Y	A	H	G	Ⓖ
■	T	S	C	Q	R	Z	U	E	R	C	F	T	L	K
U	N	Ⓡ	L	O	X	T	H	A	F	X	Z	H	V	E
R	W	E	L	Q	E	■	I	T	Ⓖ	E	V	U	U	S
Ⓖ	A	L	Ⓖ	Ⓜ	Ⓜ	N	I	A	R	Ⓖ	D	O	D	P
P	J	L	Ⓛ	Ⓦ	Ⓘ	C	H	■	E	F	X	U	O	B
O	Q	L	Ⓔ	Ⓦ	Ⓓ	E	J	Ⓡ	G	I	V	U	T	Z
V	B	F	Ⓡ	Ⓔ	■	O	A	W	R	N	I	L	L	O

G7100016

1. To make, perform, or contribute _ _ _ _ _ _ _
2. Tiger's dimpled friend _ _ _ _ _ _ _ _ _
3. A repeat show _ _ _ _ _ _
4. Dip of the Aztecs _ _ _ _ _ _ _ _ _ _
5. Twinkled, flickered **G L I M M E R E D**
6. Trustworthiness _ _ _ _ _ _ _ _ _ _ _
7. An explosive projectile _ _ _ _ _ _ _ _ _
8. Lucrative, profitable _ _ _ _ _ _ _ _
9. To determine, confirm _ _ _ _ _ _ _ _
10. National or Budget _ _ _ _ _ _ _ _ _ _
11. Energize, refresh _ _ _ _ _ _ _ _ _
12. A main attraction at amusement parks _ _ _ _ _ _ _ _ _ _ _ _ _ _ _ _
13. Europe's largest island _ _ _ _ _ _ _ _ _ _ _ _ _ _
14. A dairy farmer's slogan _ _ _ _ _ _ _ _
15. Process of thickening a sauce _ _ _ _ _ _ _ _ _
Scramble: A head of state _ _ _ _ _ _ _ _ _

A	O	R	N	I	P	S		L	A	E	W	S	E	R
I	I	D	R	P	F	W	L		C	G	D	O	B	I
S	E	D	L	M	V		M	O	D	X	H	T	H	K
N	M	F	N	N	A	H	M	R	F	S	H	V	Q	N
U	G	T	L	S	T	V	E	W	W	G	X	C	U	E
K	C	K	N	J	T	R	Y	A	Z	W	C	E	T	A
U	R		G	O	F	U	R	V	P	L	R	I	W	L
N	O	D	S	E	R	L	T	R	M	T	E	O	L	E
A	J	Q	S	W	L	K	Y	G	I	J	W	N	U	Q
N	I	H	W	H	O	A	Z	H	B	R	Z	W	P	E
G	K	I		D	N	N	I	T	H	I	T	T	O	N
C	G	A	T	I	R	E	D	U	I	X	P	Y	A	G
H	E	D	L	V	G		Y	H	H	D	X	X	L	
E	I	I	Y	R	S	A	G	B	E	U	I	I	I	F
H	R	E	R	O	U	L	M	T	T	L	I	E	I	E

A4000021

1. Good for you _ _ _ _ _ _ _
2. The natural reserves R E S O U R C E S
3. Jogging _ _ _ _ _ _ _ _
4. Dangerous trails _ _ _ _ _ _ _ _ _ _ _ _ _
5. Sunny skies, low pressure system _ _ _ _ _ _ _ _ _ _ _ _ _
6. Taking it easy, resting _ _ _ _ _ _ _ _ _
7. Be attentive for this _ _ _ _ _ _ _ _
8. Walking in a winter paradise _ _ _ _ _ _ _ _ _ _ _ _
9. Often used with a compass and GPS _ _ _ _ _ _ _ _ _ _
10. Not at sea level _ _ _ _ _ _ _ _ _ _ _ _ _
11. Will take you trotting _ _ _ _ _ _ _
12. If you're above this, you're close to the top _ _ _ _ _ _ _ _ _
13. Many trails follow this _ _ _ _ _ _
14. Walking with gear _ _ _ _ _ _ _
15. A term for trail difficulty _ _ _ _ _ _ _ _ _
Scramble: Signaling _ _ _ _ _ _ _ _ _ _

S	E	X	J	F	J	Z	R	D	N	O	U	S	T	F
L	F	N	R	P	K	S		N	C	H	P	W	W	J
K	M	I	C	H	G	B	W	S	A	D	S	R	V	I
S	L	W	Y	W		R	U	P	D	G	A	A	P	C
T	F	A	R	A	D	F	A	E	O	O	C	Q	H
S	B	I	T	N	V	U	L	X	S	T	W	T	I	B
H	B	U	P	Q	F	M	E	C	Z	G	K	S	B	E
H	D	N	S	I	E	B		R	Q	E	A	N	F
W		G	L	U	T	L	W	Y	O	L	J	Q	I
T	Y	M	X	T	A	V	E	M	Z	G	L	U	A	T
I	I	Z	N	F	E	N	T	M	Z	R	S	L	H	A
E	J	S	R	F	S	R	O	C	N	S	W	V	E	W
B	G	P	S	O	K	U	S	Y	A	G	H	D	Q	E
M	E	L	W	I	O	N	F	E	X	I	F	X	D	J
N	N	P	P	V	H	F	O		R	W	F	K	E	R

G7100019

1. Dignitary throws at the ballpark _ _ _ _ _ _ _ _ _ _ _ _ _ _
2. Golfing groups _ _ _ _ _ _ _ _ _ _
3. Lightning's partner _ _ _ _ _ _ _ _
4. For pedestrians _ _ _ _ _ _ _ _ _
5. San Diego's Mexican neighbor _ _ _ _ _ _ _ _ _
6. Red headed birds _ _ _ _ _ _ _ _ _ _
7. For Presidents and Lovers _ _ _ _ _ _ _ _ _
8. Riding streetcars _ _ _ _ _ _ _ _ _ _ _
9. The torso's narrow part _ _ _ _ _
10. Lizards with regenerating tails _ _ _ _ _ _
11. Ballads _ _ _ _ _
12. Spoken easily _ _ _ _ _ _ _ _
13. Between 999 and 1 Million _ _ _ _ _ _ _ _ _
14. Used by a train, referee, and policeman W H I S T L E
15. Home to world class wine and cheeses _ _ _ _ _ _
16. In a place _ _ _ _ _
Scramble: Francis of Assisi's namesake _ _ _ _ _ _ _ _ _ _ _ _ _

M	R	O	U	B	E	M	R	H	A	T	U	I	T	■
E	B	D	F	M	T	B	I	P	P	Q	J	N	J	G
D	C	G	M	A	C	R	F	D	S	T	B	R	A	S
T	Z	I	O	R	D	Z	W	G	E	M	K	X	Y	C
E	E	M	A	P	S	B	K	T	T	S	T	Z	O	I
T	F	P	K	M	Y	A	L	L	P	■	U	S	M	E
I	N	E	W	T	V	N	■	J	U	C	W	I	U	P
I	V	O	T	Z	D	S	G	W	R	O	M	■	T	L
U	E	R	K	P	■	■	N	I	I	M	W	O	U	R
E	A	R	U	E	Q		H	A	F	D	U	N	K	P
W	B	S	I	P	C	I	D	L	T	O	C	■	E	E
T	R	T	T	C	A	L	O	C	T	E	A	Y	T	
L	C	Q	E	N	O	Y	E	J	X	T	W	Q	M	U
O	A	O	G	U	G	H	H	O	P	H	M	E	G	X
I	A	P	R	X	F	S	R	R	N	T	R	R	D	B

A4000016

1. Movie advertisements _ _ _ _ _ _ _ _
2. The best thing for corn since being popped _ _ _ _ _ _ _ _ _ _ _ _ _ _
3. All the work and money required making a movie _ _ _ _ _ _ _ _ _ _ _ _
4. Netflix, RedBox, for example _ _ _ _ _ _ _
5. Drive-in, IMAX, and stadium seating _ _ _ _ _ _ _
6. The feeling from suspenseful or scary movies _ _ _ _ _ _ _ _ _ _
7. These "stars" can be very subjective _ _ _ _ _ _ _ _
8. Before a movie starts _ _ _ _ _ _ _ _ _
9. A movie's popular companion _ _ _ _ _ _ _
10. Movies never for the theater _ _ _ _ _ _ _ _ _ _
11. Buy the soundtrack _ _ _ _ _ _
12. A cheaper movie _ _ _ _ _ _ _ _
13. Torn when you enter _ _ _ _ _ _ _ _ _
14. Authentic or believable films R E A L I S T I C
15. Movie on a rainy day or when you're bored _ _ _ _ _ _ _ _ _ _
Scramble: The only major film studio in Hollywood _ _ _ _ _ _ _ _ _

C	I	B	K	N	T	F	F	N	S	A	S	L	A	G
A	M	L	■	I	H	A	O	H	I	F	F	N	V	W
O	H	G	O	R	L	W	E	H	Y	V	V	H	H	E
M	P	B	G	O	M	Z	U	E	Y	X	I	V	Q	L
E	N	Y	O	H	K	U	R	E	W	L	M	D	S	L
■	W	E	T	E	C	N	J	D	N	B	I	B	F	W
M	H	E	S	W	O	Q	Q	W	K	E	E	Y	L	A
C	O	S	D	P	G	D	O	N	X	N	X	A	O	B
I	R	Y	L	D	C	I	O	R	T	W	P	Z	O	E
Z	I	B	E	U	A	B	T	V	W	■	R	D	R	V
L	F	T	O	L	W	A	A	■	E	A	G	U	O	R
H	R	E	Q	T	I	C	K	R	L	C	A	R	J	W
J	A	E	W	J	N	T	X	M	E	M	B	M	W	R
P	M	M	Y	Y	V	U	W	H	Z	M	N	R	G	L
T	L	W	S	T	E	V	I	W	H	T	N	R	W	E

G7100021

1. Key concrete ingredient _ _ _ _ _ _ _ _ _ _
2. A Dutch symbol _ _ _ _ _ _ _ _ _
3. A hayride _ _ _ _ _ _ _ _ _ _
4. Italian sports car _ _ _ _ _ _ _ _ _ _ _ _
5. An MLB team's goal _ _ _ _ _ _ _ _ _ _ _ _
6. Expressed on paper **W R I T T E N**
7. Brand of jeans popular with cowboys _ _ _ _ _ _ _ _ _
8. A southpaw _ _ _ _ _ _ _ _ _ _ _
9. The "gentler sex" _ _ _ _ _ _
10. From the tanning of animal hides _ _ _ _ _ _ _ _
11. A popular gum flavor _ _ _ _ _ _ _ _ _ _ _ _ _
12. Forbes spotlights this _ _ _ _ _ _ _
13. Sin City _ _ _ _ _ _ _ _ _
14. Riga is this country's capital _ _ _ _ _ _ _
15. Symbolic end of summer in the US _ _ _ _ _ _ _ _ _
Scramble: Meals _ _ _ _ _ _ _ _

C	Z	U	R	F	S	M	T	E	X	R	P	K	C	O
S	E	X	I	P	K	R	A	M	O	R	J	Y	E	N
N	O	H	O	H	N	H	G	S	T	W	Q	E	P	A
L	N	J	B	C	L	R	S	K	I	Z	F	F	D	K
O	I	P	D	E	Z	X	B	E	X	C	U	K	O	P
	E	O	H	R	I	V	J	K	O	E	W	C	K	E
S	E	V	L	F	H	N	A	B	T	M	C	M	C	V
C	L	E	S	T	Y	W		U	C	B	V	R	F	F
O	Y	J	L	F	C	L	I	D	R	G	A	C	O	
B	E	P	G	C		D	W	H	G	A	F	V	R	L
Q		B	G	P	R	I	O	H	E	R	F	U	K	S
O	H	D	A	F	A	T	N	S	H	T	S	E	Q	L
C	L	Q	U	M	N	R	Z	E	C	I	U	D	C	N
A	I	I	S	A	N	I	F	B	A	S	S	S	C	I
C	K	H	Y	W	C	T	E	T	I	F	R		I	E

A4000020

1. School lunches unite **C A F E T E R I A**
2. A time to eat with these _ _ _ _ _ _ _
3. Preferred in the form of roll-ups _ _ _ _ _ _ _
4. Starbucks _ _ _ _ _ _ _ _ _ _
5. Each pays the bill for their food _ _ _ _ _ _ _ _ _
6. Drive-thru _ _ _ _ _ _ _ _
7. Brown Bag-It _ _ _ _ _ _ _ _ _ _
8. No checks accepted _ _ _ _ _ _ _ _ _ _ _
9. Only the best food from a potato _ _ _ _ _ _ _ _ _ _ _ _ _ _
10. PB and J, Bologna, etc. _ _ _ _ _ _ _ _ _
11. Food for the body _ _ _ _ _ _
12. Kids don't like to do this with yummy snacks _ _ _ _ _
13. Clip this to save money _ _ _ _ _ _ _
14. When it's your birthday or anniversary _ _ _ _ _ _ _ _ _ _ _ _
15. A growling stomach _ _ _ _ _ _ _ _
16. Instant soup _ _ _ _ _ _ _ _ _ _ _ _
Scramble: Dutch _ _ _ _ _ _ _ _ _ _

Difficulty: ★★☆☆☆

H	S	S	C	O	S	R	I	Y	V	■	N	E	L	M
C	X	V	V	A	D	X	O	B	V	L	C	F	U	U
B	K	J	U	I	U	J	O	Ⓘ	U	N	X	S	E	H
Z	N	O	K	U	V	E	P	Ⓝ	A	■	T	T	P	R
I	X	V	F	H	I	T	Q	N	U	R	S	A	D	I
W	Ⓔ	B	E	S	E	D	M	X	B	C	B	D	N	N
T	K	I	■	J	C	U	Ⓑ	Ⓔ	H	G	S	Z	K	I
Ⓑ	F	X	C	A	E	T	F	R	■	R	D	D	D	Ⓑ
O	T	V	P	E	Ⓝ	■	E	V	N	M	I	L	F	L
F	W	I	M	R	E	G	A	Ⓝ	Y	A	X	M	L	O
N	E	■	Ⓔ	Ⓘ	H	R	Q	O	G	M	M	P	Ⓔ	■
J	Ⓡ	Ⓑ	I	Z	T	Q	B	E	A	N	Ⓘ	O	K	K
I	Ⓤ	Ⓝ	N	Y	I	U	T	H	U	L	G	R	E	Y
Ⓔ	Ⓤ	Ⓖ	G	Y	P	T	Y	Z	Q	I	P	O	W	H
E	Ⓘ	Ⓓ	■	N	N	■	N	W	Ⓘ	A	C	S	A	E

G7100031

1. Strength and vigor _ _ _ _ _ _
2. Musical tool _ _ _ _ _ _ _ _ _ _ _
3. Popular yachting color _ _ _ _ _ _ _ _ _
4. CEO or VP _ _ _ _ _ _ _ _ _ _ _
5. A span, connection **B R I D G E**
6. Airline ticket _ _ _ _ _ _ _ _ _ _ _ _ _ _
7. Master bedroom _ _ _ _ _ _ _ _
8. Certain, inevitable _ _ _ _ _ _ _ _ _
9. Baseball's period _ _ _ _ _ _ _
10. Dictatorship above the 38th parallel _ _ _ _ _ _ _ _ _ _ _
11. Scotland's capital _ _ _ _ _ _ _ _ _ _
12. Lizards inhabiting the Galapagos _ _ _ _ _ _ _ _
13. Baseball skipper at first or third _ _ _ _ _ _ _ _ _ _
14. Displays, spectacles _ _ _ _ _ _ _ _ _ _ _ _
15. Common workday _ _ _ _ _ _ _ _ _ _
16. One or the other _ _ _ _ _ _ _
Scramble: Adversary _ _ _ _ _ _ _ _

R	K	Y	S	U	■	G	O	L	N	U	R	I	N	O
C	T	D	S	X	T	D	C	O	O	B	P	H	C	R
J	K	H	O	Z	I	N	A	T	A	U	L	Y	G	T
R	X	H	C	S	I	L	E	E	■	N	W	N	C	A
A	G	S	B	■	A	F	B	T	T	G	R	T	C	O
■	D	V	U	K	I	L	R	S	O	M	H	W	T	K
S	U	P	M	C	G	D	H	T	F	P	C	F	O	J
E	L	H	R	G	D	D	V	I	■	C	U	C	C	B
O	R	L	W	E	R	A	S	O	K	J	C	V	F	Z
U	P	B	A	N	■	A	D	E	T	A	U	U	T	K
R	T	■	Q	E	S	S	I	R	I	N	M	W	C	M
C	I	S	C	H	C	N	M	Q	O	O	F	L	■	N
A	G	C	L	W	G	R	X	T	M	W	Z	Y	I	Q
L	Q	A	N	A	N	T	T	T	U	U	I	J	P	O
P	G	N	G	U	I	A	F	C	W	E	W	P	N	G

A4000006

1. Take advantage of this special lane _ _ _ _ _ _ _
2. Braking, cussing, swerving, and gesturing are examples of this _ _ _ _ _ _ _ _ _
3. Never a good time for this _ _ _ _ _ _ _ _ _ _ _
4. Usually red in front of you the whole way to and from work _ _ _ _ _ _ _ _ _ _ _
5. Move the lever either up or down _ _ _ _ _ _ _
6. The common time to and from work _ _ _ _ _ _ _ _ _ _
7. The avg. person spends 35 minutes a day doing this <u>C O M M U T I N G</u>
8. These cause severe traffic backups _ _ _ _ _ _ _
9. Used to take a car off the road _ _ _ _ _ _ _ _
10. Cussing usually follows this common traffic violation _ _ _ _ _ _ _
11. Creates a need to call the office from your car _ _ _ _ _ _ _ _ _ _ _ _ _
12. A commuter's companion _ _ _ _ _ _
13. Please use your turn signal when doing this! _ _ _ _ _ _ _ _ _ _ _ _ _ _
14. The feeling usually found after a long commute _ _ _ _ _ _
15. Can happen in the snow or mud _ _ _ _ _ _
16. This is essential when blizzards hit _ _ _ _ _ _ _ _ _ _ _
17. Most cars have this "control" _ _ _ _ _ _ _ _ _
Scramble: Bumper to bumper _ _ _ _ _ _ _ _ _

Difficulty: ★★⯪☆☆

D	E	H	B	O	S	(H)	C	I	E	N	E	B	O	S
J	H	H	E	(N)	U	U	A	H	U	U	V	L	O	E
W	I	Q	D	E	L	K	D	W	T	H	S	(P)	R	M
(P)	J	O	R	S	C	C	X	B	E	C	N	J	O	R
(T)	(A)	W	H	V	O	C	Y	(N)	T	S	(H)	G	P	O
(T)		P	D	Q	Y	(O)	R	A	(I)		O	T	S	A
(S)	(E)	E	R	E	Y		I	B	L	E	L	R	L	(P)
G	E		G	O	O	R	A	B	N	S	(N)		O	
H	T	N	H	(I)	R	Q	U	G	E	W	X	N	L	S
R	T	(H)	W	A	N	F	M	M	W	T	R	T	P	P
A	F	L	E	K	R	U	W	B	M	C	U	N	Z	Z
	O	(P)	S	N	J	A	S	A	L	(H)	N	I	J	E
L	I	P	A	E	O	D	Y	P	Z	A	V	R	S	I
I	G	C	I	O	O	I	B	A	E	E	K	X	I	G
U	P	(I)	T	F	L	E	(H)	N	D	R	O	M	E	N

G7100035

1. Calculus' antiderivative _ _ _ _ _ _ _ _ _
2. The Hunchback of Dame _ _ _ _ _ _
3. To inhabit or colonize _ _ _ _ _ _ _ _ _ _
4. Europe's second largest island _ _ _ _ _ _ _ _
5. Laughing Canines _ _ _ _ _ _ _
6. Used to make music _ _ _ _ _ _ _ _ _ _ _ _
7. An embarrassing or uncomfortable situation **H O T S E A T**
8. Big trouble; a can of worms _ _ _ _ _ _ _ _ _ _ _ _ _
9. Not the driver _ _ _ _ _ _ _ _ _ _ _
10. Not melodies _ _ _ _ _ _ _ _ _ _
11. A successful team year after year _ _ _ _ _ _ _ _ _ _ _ _ _
12. Frank Sinatra's birthplace _ _ _ _ _ _ _ _ _ _
13. Largest lake and country in Central America _ _ _ _ _ _ _ _ _ _
14. A question or issue _ _ _ _ _ _ _ _
15. McDonald's staple _ _ _ _ _ _ _ _ _
Scramble: Textiles, railroads, and steel _ _ _ _ _ _ _ _ _ _ _

Difficulty: ★★⯨☆☆   PUZZLE 49: **Vacation**

O	Ⓡ	R	■	T	B	C	N	T	A	R	T	O	R	Ⓕ
A	L	P	X	A	Ⓡ	U	E	P	J	O	Z	K	G	U
O	Y	X	U	K	Z	K	Ⓢ	E	N	H	U	V	Y	A
O	F	B	S	Q	E	A	N	N	I	H	■	S	I	■
X	C	A	E	J	M	V	C	T	N	K	U	S	Z	P
W	R	T	R	M	D	M	I	V	N	Ⓕ	Ⓕ	E	T	W
A	Y	D	F	K	Ⓕ	P	P	H	W	B	E	T	J	O
P	I	C	T	I	I	N	R	■	U	Q	S	Ⓜ	Ⓞ	■
H	■	H	U	N	R	N	F	S	N	D	Ⓔ	Q	Ⓡ	
G	E	F	C	Z	L	P	B	O	O	X	Y	Ⓔ	Ⓓ	Ⓕ
S	A	W	C	Ⓢ	B	U	Ⓢ	O	C	A	S	N	Q	I
G	I	E	G	N	T	A	N	A	U	Ⓡ	Ⓕ	J	A	X
K	Ⓢ	N	P	E	V	R	G	F	T	F	A	Y	B	R
G	S	E	E	Ⓡ	E	■	R	L	D	E	D	L	L	U
H	T	E	L	V	I	M	N	E	I	B	Ⓡ	G	S	E

A4000023

1. Hit the slopes! _ _ _ _ _ _ _ _
2. Compact or Luxury _ _ _ _ _ _ _ _ _ _
3. The feeling when you're not chained to your desk **F R E E D O M**
4. Sea shore _ _ _ _ _ _ _ _ _ _ _
5. Take the RV or station wagon _ _ _ _ _ _ _ _ _ _ _
6. Lucky _ _ _ _ _ _ _ _ _
7. Renew, refresh _ _ _ _ _ _ _ _ _ _
8. Many funny looking lines from these _ _ _ _ _ _ _ _
9. Tradition _ _ _ _ _ _ _
10. A repeatable, enjoyable place _ _ _ _ _ _ _ _ _ _ _ _ _
11. Done with cameras and fanny packs _ _ _ _ _ _ _ _ _ _ _ _
12. Save up! _ _ _ _ _ _ _ _ _
13. Fees for public transportation _ _ _ _ _ _
14. Often the main reason for beach vacations _ _ _ _ _ _ _ _
15. Hanging out and enjoying the beach _ _ _ _ _ _ _ _ _ _ _ _ _
Scramble: Usually 15, 30, or 45 _ _ _ _ _ _ _ _ _ _

Difficulty: ★★☆☆☆

A	A	K	U	K	H	Q	F	V	Z	O	C	A	W	L
D	A	T	M	H	Q	M	A	Y	I	M	G	M	N	K
D	R	P	P	A	U	R	Z	E	N	L	N	F	I	L
K	I	X	Q	H	X	D	R		E	H	X	U	N	X
C	U	I	E	D	K	T	N	T	X	P	X	H	W	J
M	E	X	O	M	U	Q	A	E	R	N	C	P	B	A
V	R	G	Q	O	I	Q	J	V	S	A	X	R	O	
U	A	G	J	F			O	F	Y	U	C	L	F	E
O	F	G	S	G	I	T	W	T	D	R	E	C	F	K
U	H	C	R	I	E	O	O	Y	T	U	X	B	S	Q
S	J	S	D	X	N	Z	T		X	L	E	F	T	K
T	G	D	S	B	X	U	E	L	L	B	C	O	R	E
V	B	L	I	M	F	V	F	I	Q	G	T	R	S	P
V	I	M	F	Z	T	N	Z	O	U	N	R	U	N	O
K	Q	I	T	S	E	Q	S	X	I	I	T	A	N	E

G7100046

1. Carrying, moving _ _ _ _ _ _ _ _ _ _ _ _ _
2. Don of La Mancha _ _ _ _ _ _ _ _
3. Host of *Pimp My Ride* _ _ _ _ _ _ _
4. Home to Nikes and Reeboks at the mall _ _ _ _ _ _ _ _ _ _ _ _
5. Arrow holders _ _ _ _ _ _ _ _
6. Females have two, males have one _ _ _ _ _ _ _ _ _ _ _ _
7. Logo, brand _ _ _ _ _ _ _ _ _ _
8. Administrator, executor **T R U S T E E**
9. Division's result _ _ _ _ _ _ _ _ _
10. The Truth is Out There _ _ _ _ _ _ _
11. Many a teenager's dream _ _ _ _ _ _ _ _ _ _ _
12. Mathematical squares _ _ _ _ _ _ _ _ _
13. Chair for a king _ _ _ _ _ _ _
14. Anxiety and panic pharmaceutical _ _ _ _ _ _
15. A new couple's pleasant emotional journey _ _ _ _ _ _ _ _ _ _ _ _ _ _ _ _
Scramble: Amusement park staples _ _ _ _ _ _ _ _ _ _ _ _

O	J	X	V	L	G	Q	C	D	I	T	G	I	R	S
Q	O	N	L	C	L	N	E	A	U	L	H	P	M	T
D	B	H	U	D	D	J	C	I	H	B	F	R	R	L
F	Z	Y	H	X	G	W	F	P	E	X	S	N	O	S
C	I	Y	A	G	Y	T	C	Q	K	Y	U	T	O	A
J	C	O	A	F	M	E	M	E	R	E	A	W	B	B
R	F	Q	E	I	S		W	L	I	A	K	T	R	E
	E	A	N	Z	C	A	E	O	N	O	R	V	M	T
E	I	H	L	I	E	E		G	R	C	E	Y	R	S
X		Q	S	Z	W	R	E	N	B	I	S	L	O	
S	O	V	M	R	B	A	D	A	B	P	B	I	H	L
E	O	T	S	M	T	E		S	C	G	J	V	N	U
E	G	E	C	B		N	D		E	P	C	K	M	L
E	Z	V	A	H	C	L	M	B	N	K	H	W	D	W
R	A		R	U	T	E	E	R	A	F	L	N	B	I

A4000022

1. For the peach and champagne lover! _ _ _ _ _ _ _ _
2. Green alternative to lemonade _ _ _ _ _ _ _ _
3. Fruity milkshakes _ _ _ _ _ _ _ _ _ _
4. A "type of wine" _ _ _ _ _ _ _
5. Best "on tap" _ _ _ _ _ _
6. A chilled wine concoction _ _ _ _ _ _ _
7. A popular bar marketing event _ _ _ _ _ _ _ _ _ _ _ _ _
8. Found mixing the drinks _ _ _ _ _ _ _ _ _
9. An orange juice and cream drink _ _ _ _ _ _ _ _ _ _ _
10. A drink **B E V E R A G E**
11. A popular flavor or a garnish _ _ _ _ _ _ _ _ _ _
12. A sauce, sprinkles, shavings, and more _ _ _ _ _ _ _ _ _ _ _
13. A spiked iced tea _ _ _ _ _ _ _ _ _ _ _
14. Brandy and whiskey _ _ _ _ _ _ _ _
15. Tall, Venti or Grande? _ _ _ _ _ _ _
Scramble: A southern brewed favorite _ _ _ _ _ _ _ _

Difficulty: ★★☆☆☆

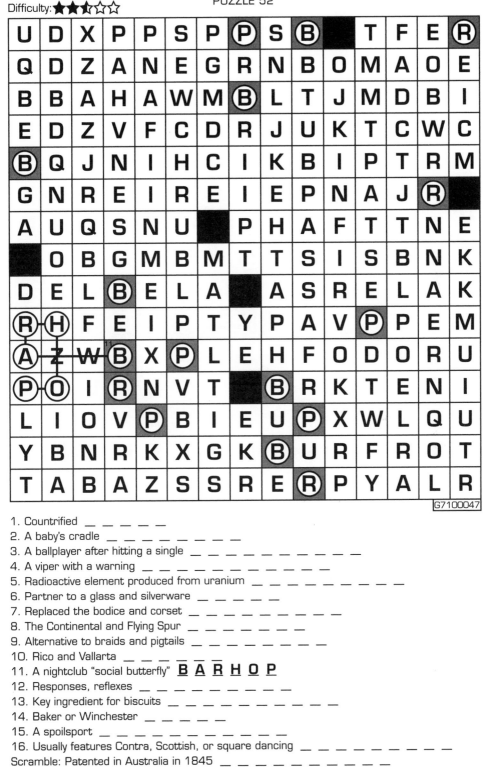

U	D	X	P	P	S	P	Ⓟ	S	Ⓑ		T	F	E	Ⓡ
Q	D	Z	A	N	E	G	R	N	B	O	M	A	O	E
B	B	A	H	A	W	M	Ⓑ	L	T	J	M	D	B	I
E	D	Z	V	F	C	D	R	J	U	K	T	C	W	C
Ⓑ	Q	J	N	I	H	C	I	K	B	I	P	T	R	M
G	N	R	E	I	R	E	I	E	P	N	A	J	Ⓡ	
A	U	Q	S	N	U		P	H	A	F	T	T	N	E
	O	B	G	M	B	M	T	T	S	I	S	B	N	K
D	E	L	Ⓑ	E	L	A		A	S	R	E	L	A	K
Ⓡ	Ⓗ	F	E	I	P	T	Y	P	A	V	Ⓟ	P	E	M
Ⓐ	Z	W	Ⓑ	X	Ⓟ	L	E	H	F	O	D	O	R	U
Ⓟ	Ⓞ	I	Ⓡ	N	V	T		Ⓑ	R	K	T	E	N	I
L	I	O	V	Ⓟ	B	I	E	U	Ⓟ	X	W	L	Q	U
Y	B	N	R	K	X	G	K	Ⓑ	U	R	F	R	O	T
T	A	B	A	Z	S	S	R	E	Ⓡ	P	Y	A	L	R

G7100047

1. Countrified _ _ _ _ _
2. A baby's cradle _ _ _ _ _ _ _ _
3. A ballplayer after hitting a single _ _ _ _ _ _ _ _ _ _ _
4. A viper with a warning _ _ _ _ _ _ _ _ _ _ _
5. Radioactive element produced from uranium _ _ _ _ _ _ _ _ _ _
6. Partner to a glass and silverware _ _ _ _ _ _
7. Replaced the bodice and corset _ _ _ _ _ _ _ _ _ _
8. The Continental and Flying Spur _ _ _ _ _ _ _
9. Alternative to braids and pigtails _ _ _ _ _ _ _ _ _
10. Rico and Vallarta _ _ _ _ _
11. A nightclub "social butterfly" B A R H O P
12. Responses, reflexes _ _ _ _ _ _ _ _ _
13. Key ingredient for biscuits _ _ _ _ _ _ _ _ _ _
14. Baker or Winchester _ _ _ _ _
15. A spoilsport _ _ _ _ _ _ _ _ _ _ _
16. Usually features Contra, Scottish, or square dancing _ _ _ _ _ _ _ _ _
Scramble: Patented in Australia in 1845 _ _ _ _ _ _ _ _ _ _

Ⓕ	P	A	T	I	Ⓢ	X	H	T	D	F	S	L	C	L
E	V	A	I	B		R	O	I	C	W	V	X	J	S
I	O	B	N	T	A	B	M	G	K	F	D	X	V	S
H	P	F	U	E	U	R	Y	N	Q	I	V	U	Ⓕ	R
H	J	S	A		G	T	F	D	I	Ⓛ O Ⓔ	H	Ⓢ
	M	Q	W	O		Ⓕ	E	E	G	I	L	F	G	K
E	L	O	B	Ⓒ	U	T	O	Ⓒ X P T	Ⓢ	A	N
C	W	N	W	E	Y	N	N	M	Ⓜ Ⓑ	M	Ⓕ	W	L
H	I	N	O	R	A	Y	Q	Ⓡ Ⓐ	R	G	Z	P	A
J	K	V	P	Ⓢ	S	A	M		Ⓢ	D	Ⓒ	T	U	E
A	R	S	P	B	G	E	S	C	Z	E	Ⓒ	A	I	Y
D	D	S	C	Ⓢ	A	M	M	I	L	U	C	D	C	D
A	T	Q	N	B	I	U	F	O	Ⓒ	S	V	N	D	I
R	J	N	Ⓕ	E	R	S	U	M	L	E	M	G	Z	R
O	N	E	Z	Y	N	A	B	H	C	Ⓕ	O	A	S	S

A4000012

1. The hardest part to maintain _ _ _ _ _ _ _ _ _ _
2. The first half _ _ _ _ _ _ _ _ _
3. Often heard from fellow golfers _ _ _ _ _ _ _ _
4. A format for selecting the best ball **S C R A M B L E**
5. Your directional indicator _ _ _ _ _ _ _ _ _ _
6. Needed along with determination _ _ _ _ _
7. Found at the start, the turn, and the end of the round _ _ _ _ _ _ _ _ _ _
8. When someone wants to win _ _ _ _ _ _ _ _ _ _ _ _ _
9. Tiger Woods became this _ _ _ _ _ _ _
10. Money bet on every hole _ _ _ _ _ _ _ _ _ _ _
11. A ball hard right or left _ _ _ _ _ _ _ _
12. Used off the tee _ _ _ _ _ _ _ _ _
13. Looking the part _ _ _ _ _ _ _ _ _ _ _ _
14. Cut across the ball _ _ _ _ _ _ _
15. They carry your bag _ _ _ _ _ _
16. The moment of truth after each hole _ _ _ _ _ _ _ _ _ _ _ _
Scramble: Friendly, good fellowship _ _ _ _ _ _ _ _ _ _ _

Difficulty: ★★⯨☆☆

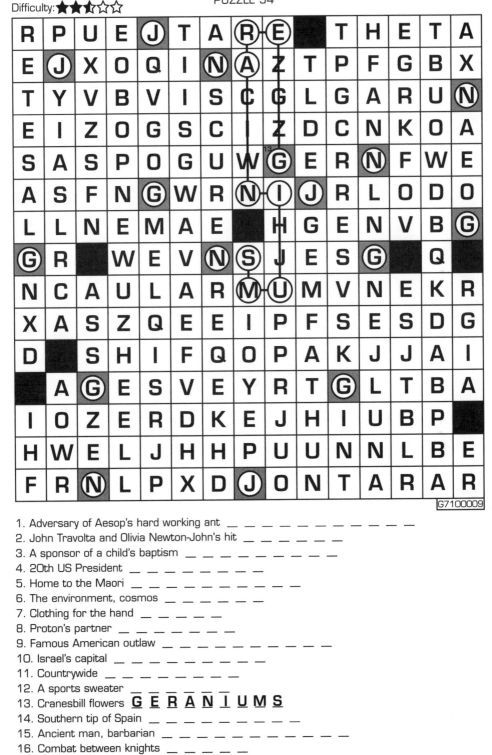

R	P	U	E	J	T	A	R	E		T	H	E	T	A
E	J	X	O	Q	I	N	A	Z	T	P	F	G	B	X
T	Y	V	B	V	I	S	C	G	L	G	A	R	U	N
E	I	Z	O	G	S	C	Z	D	C	N	K	O	A
S	A	S	P	O	G	U	W	G	E	R	N	F	W	E
A	S	F	N	G	W	R	N	I	J	R	L	O	D	O
L	L	N	E	M	A	E		H	G	E	N	V	B	G
G	R		W	E	V	N	S	J	E	S	G		Q
N	C	A	U	L	A	R	M	U	M	V	N	E	K	R
X	A	S	Z	Q	E	E	I	P	F	S	E	S	D	G
D		S	H	I	F	Q	O	P	A	K	J	J	A	I
	A	G	E	S	V	E	Y	R	T	G	L	T	B	A
I	O	Z	E	R	D	K	E	J	H	I	U	B	P
H	W	E	L	J	H	H	P	U	U	N	N	L	B	E
F	R	N	L	P	X	D	J	O	N	T	A	R	A	R

G7100009

1. Adversary of Aesop's hard working ant _ _ _ _ _ _ _ _ _ _ _ _
2. John Travolta and Olivia Newton-John's hit _ _ _ _ _ _ _
3. A sponsor of a child's baptism _ _ _ _ _ _ _ _ _ _
4. 20th US President _ _ _ _ _ _ _ _
5. Home to the Maori _ _ _ _ _ _ _ _ _ _
6. The environment, cosmos _ _ _ _ _ _
7. Clothing for the hand _ _ _ _ _
8. Proton's partner _ _ _ _ _ _ _
9. Famous American outlaw _ _ _ _ _ _ _ _ _ _ _
10. Israel's capital _ _ _ _ _ _ _ _ _ _
11. Countrywide _ _ _ _ _ _ _ _
12. A sports sweater _ _ _ _ _ _
13. Cranesbill flowers G E R A N I U M S
14. Southern tip of Spain _ _ _ _ _ _ _ _ _ _
15. Ancient man, barbarian _ _ _ _ _ _ _ _ _ _ _
16. Combat between knights _ _ _ _ _
Scramble: A clown _ _ _ _ _ _ _

E	N	(A)	Y	P	R	N	Q	A	O	C	J	U	M	H
G	M	R	L	R	M	H	K	L	W	Z	N	W	U	Z
E	B	N	P	B	T	O	E	■	Z	Y	H	D	A	Y
■	I	T	B	U	E	B	J	H	A	P	I	(W)	O	O
O	D	E	C	Z	X	Y	T	G	K	U	E	C	(E)	(L)
B	V	L	F	V	O	Y	V	(C)	S	G	(A)	F	P	(M)
A	X	(W)	Z	S	X	I	R	(W)	(A)	Z	L	I	H	F
R	O	S	E	S	R	(P)	L	A	L	E	H	(P)	(T)	(S)
R	E	D	N	■	P	N	N	L	R	I	Z	F	I	C
■	(P)	A	S	A	P	A	Q	O	C	E	B	U	O	J
T	M	Q	S	W	E	E	K	S	P	L	N	D	R	I
D	F	E	A	I	R	V	(W)	■	D	(C)	G	C	T	(P)
A	R	J	B	E	A	B	H	(P)	R	A	■	A	T	R
R	M	P	V	O	D	Q	M	H	■	I	X	S	A	T
■	T	C	(C)	N	U	E	I	T	(C)	R	A	N	A	I

G7000022

1. Past NFL Lineman _ _ _ _ _ _ _ _ _ _ _ _
2. The female judge _ _ _ _ _ _ _ _ _ _
3. Kelly Monaco and Toni Braxton's partner _ _ _ _ _ _ _ _ _
4. Each celebrity's partner _ _ _ _ _ _ _ _ _ _ _ _
5. The "Spanish Bullfight" dance _ _ _ _ _ _ _ _ _ _ _ _
6. A ballroom dance _ _ _ _ _ _
7. Great dancing race car driver _ _ _ _ _ _ _ _ _ _ _ _
8. Third place dancer, de la Fuente _ _ _ _ _ _ _ _ _
9. A score of 30 _ _ _ _ _ _ _ _
10. The Tango from Season 8 _ _ _ _ _ _ _ _ _
11. Conclusion for Misty May-Treanor, Sara Evans, and Jewel _ _ _ _ _ _ _ _ _
12. Lisa Rinna, Monique Coleman, and Trista Sutter's Partner A M S T E L
13. Apple's dancing nerd _ _ _ _ _ _ _ _
14. Rehearsing _ _ _ _ _ _ _ _ _ _ _
15. Partner to Drew Lachey, Emmitt Smith, and Gilles Marini _ _ _ _ _ _ _ _ _ _
16. Source for part of the judging _ _ _ _ _ _ _
Scramble: Misty May-Treanor's injury _ _ _ _ _ _ _ _

Difficulty: ★★✫☆☆

K	U	A	K	A	M	O	P	■	P	E	■	O	D	K
O	Q	T	O	B	L	E	■	S	I	G	E	H	U	H
E	A	T	■	U	M	C	Q	N	O	W	Q	M	Q	O
■	O	U	A	A	H	R	E	■	I	K	Y	A	O	
S	C	N	L	X	G	F	L	I	P	M	G	A	Z	G
T	U	I	E	A	D	A	R	W	U	E	U	R	D	U
E	K	T	H	K	U	J	S	L	T	S	K	N	U	O
U	H	C	V	I	M	B	■	Y	O	G	E	X	E	V
V	A	U	T	N	C	S	A	D	M	O	C	E	J	L
K	U	G	Q	R	M	Q	W	Q	R	M	K	E	N	K
■	R	B	S	U	L	E	K	D	J	N	■	N	U	E
G	R	E	■	K	L	W	E	A	L	Q	U	R	T	I
V	E	C	T	N	D	O	Q	D	A	W	S	V	K	U
D	F	Y	K	Y	E	P	F	S	C	U	M	W	O	B
L	I	R	K	X	U	Z	U	■	O	K	K	T	L	A

G7100022

1. Items, components _ _ _ _ _
2. French fries' best friend _ _ _ _ _ _ _
3. What librarians often scream _ _ _ _ _ _
4. For holding arrows _ _ _ _ _ _ _ _
5. Customary _ _ _ _ _ _
6. Short, plump, German sausage **K N O C K W U R S T**
7. The result of division _ _ _ _ _ _ _ _ _
8. The famous tissue _ _ _ _ _ _ _ _
9. Asked by interviewers _ _ _ _ _ _ _ _ _
10. Venomous lizard _ _ _ _ _ _ _ _ _ _ _ _ _
11. Truth or facts accumulated over time _ _ _ _ _ _ _ _ _ _
12. Container to boil or cook foods _ _ _ _ _ _ _
13. A parasol _ _ _ _ _ _ _ _
14. Personification of the US _ _ _ _ _ _ _ _ _
15. Eucalyptus leaf lovers _ _ _ _ _ _ _
16. The Florida state pie _ _ _ _ _ _ _ _ _ _ _
Scramble: A violent disturbance or change _ _ _ _ _ _ _ _ _

Difficulty: ★★½☆☆

PUZZLE 57: **Marriage**

T	V	K	E	I	F	S	(A)	Y	D	O	P	H	Z	I
E	D	R	(P)	K	V	O	R	A	G	T	Y	D	D	H
F	I	J	X	T	J	O	X	D	U	R	E	(C)	E	B
U	A	J	A	(C)	J	B	D	E	U	F	S	(E)	I	T
H	P	H	(P)	(P)	R	R	T	H	M	L	E	T	M	■
E	R	L	G	Y	L	F	P	(C)	G	(O)	L	M	R	O
T	C	U	J	Q	E	K	J	H	T	L	R	Y	(P)	P
S	■	S	L	A	L	U	V	(A)	C	O	O	(W)	G	Y
R	B	I	L	■	L	I	L	X	U	(S)	C	(E)	I	W
U	V	Z	Q	N	C	Z	M	B	R	■	N	O	R	I
B	D	G	F	Q	W	N	P	I	M	W	O	(C)	R	E
A	A	(A)	E	S	E	T	A	T	I	H	F	Y	H	N
O	B	G	I	E	X	(C)	(A)	E	W	K	F	I	U	U
U	U	F	C	O	N	Q	I	E	M	P	R	H	D	I
N	T	C	A	C	G	A	T	N	(P)	Z	A	I	D	L

A4000010

1. Maintaining a happy attitude _ _ _ _ _ _ _ _ _
2. The roles when children arrive _ _ _ _ _ _ _ _ _ _
3. Verbal compliments and lifting up of your spouse _ _ _ _ _ _ _ _ _ _ _ _ _
4. Housework or yard work _ _ _ _ _
5. To place importance on particular items _ _ _ _ _ _ _ _ _ _ _
6. Some want them, and some do not _ _ _ _ _ _ _ _
7. A cause of divorce _ _ _ _ _ _ _ _ _
8. Professions _ _ _ _ _ _ _
9. Answerable and responsible for your actions _ _ _ _ _ _ _ _ _ _ _
10. On a "honey-do" list _ _ _ _ _ _ _ _ _ _
11. Amazing or cool A W E S O M E
12. Good help for marriage _ _ _ _ _ _ _ _ _ _ _
13. Have fun together! _ _ _ _ _ _ _ _
14. Popular for Valentine's, Birthdays, and Anniversaries _ _ _ _ _
Scramble: Parental power _ _ _ _ _ _ _ _ _ _

J	E	W	W	Q	K	X	D	O	T	L	I	K	S	J
U	U	E	R	U	P	H	A	C	C	L	U	Q	J	A
O	U	S	R	H	I	E	M	R	A	H	G	C	J	A
I	J	A	L	S	Z	V	D	H	T	M	A		O	
E	J	N	B	B	T	X	H	Q	R	B	A	I	F	L
L	C	G	A	J	N	T	A	C	S	A	E	V	N	V
N	C	G	H	W	O	X	T	U	F	V	A	E	J	L
P	G	A	E	N		I	C		E	X	K		T	U
Q	A	C	Q	F	K	R	P	F	T	S	E	R	E	V
E	M	Y	C	A	O	F	J	G	E	H	V	N	Y	A
	P	A	D	L	E	I	W	N	R	Y	R	W	Z	A
V	N	E	P		L	L		S	A	O	Z	B	B	J
P	E	C	Q	I	P	A	T	E	L	N	N	T	B	B
Z	O	N	S	E	Y		Y	A	Z	N	U	I	G	G
I	R	M	X	H	E	W	N		R	G	E	J	K	U

G7100023

1. Reading, writing and . . . _ _ _ _ _ _ _ _ _ _ _ _

2. Reptile found in China and the southeastern US **A L L I G A T O R**

3. A large, destructive force or object _ _ _ _ _ _ _ _ _ _ _

4. Particularly _ _ _ _ _ _ _ _ _ _

5. Birthplace of democracy _ _ _ _ _ _ _

6. Mandibles _ _ _ _ _ _ _ _

7. This country's music symbol is the tango _ _ _ _ _ _ _ _ _ _

8. Symbolized by diamond rings _ _ _ _ _ _ _ _

9. Chock-full _ _ _ _ _ _ _ _ _

10. Measured in degrees or radians _ _ _ _ _ _

11. The atmosphere, surroundings _ _ _ _ _ _ _ _ _ _ _ _

12. Largest city in Florida _ _ _ _ _ _ _ _ _ _ _ _ _

13. He wore the Technicolor Dreamcoat _ _ _ _ _ _

14. San Fran in 1906 and Indonesia in 2004 _ _ _ _ _ _ _ _ _ _ _ _ _

15. The flowers bloom and the birds sing _ _ _ _ _ _ _ _ _ _ _

Scramble: Oil rich peninsula _ _ _ _ _ _ _

S	U	U	M	S	(P)	S	(D)	I	K	M	V	I	M	T
J	Y	V	H	A	A	H	E	N	V	N	U	U	H	A
L	K	I	R	G	B	I	O	P	(D)	K	I	O	N	F
A	G	P	D	N	W	D	X	R	X	D	E	■	I	S
R	E	■	T	F	A	U	N	■	(P)	L	P	O	E	P
L	E	I	J	L	I	(D)	■	O	R	E	G	P	K	N
B	Z	I	M	D	G	Q	F	G	Y	(P)	T	T	V	E
(D)	L	C	U	Y	■	R	A	X	R	M	B	E	R	O
R	V	F	D	P	L	S	V	(D)	V	D	A	P	D	V
J	Z	A	I	(D)	E	R	K	L	M	G	R	N	D	T
O	P	(P)	E	M	Y	D	S	■	T	Z	C	P	W	S
P	D	I	F	N	(P)	U	(O)	(I)	■	E	W	(D)	S	O
P	C	H	Q	C	(O)	G	Q	(T)	(P)	R	U	E	J	L
T	O	E	L	E	E	H	(O)	K	O	E	B	V	■	O
E	O	B	R	■	Y	(D)	(N)	T	R	■	(P)	E	S	L

G7000021

1. Constricting plant _ _ _ _ _ _ _ _ _ _ _ _
2. Object used for transportation _ _ _ _ _ _ _ _
3. Veritaserum and Wolfsbane, for example **P O T I O N**
4. They perform a deadly kiss _ _ _ _ _ _ _ _ _ _
5. Source of Wizarding News _ _ _ _ _ _ _ _ _ _ _ _ _ _
6. Antioch, Cadmus and Ignotus _ _ _ _ _ _ _ _ _ _
7. Trelawney's class _ _ _ _ _ _ _ _ _ _ _ _
8. An animal protector _ _ _ _ _ _ _ _
9. Corruptive Magic _ _ _ _ _ _ _ _
10. The only wizard Voldemort feared _ _ _ _ _ _ _ _ _ _ _
11. For storing memories _ _ _ _ _ _ _ _ _
12. Hogwarts' Triwizard Tournament champion _ _ _ _ _ _ _
13. The boy who lived _ _ _ _ _ _ _
14. Harry's muggle family _ _ _ _ _ _ _ _ _
15. Librarian of Hogwarts _ _ _ _ _ _
Scramble: Matron in charge of the hospital wing _ _ _ _ _ _ _ _

S	R	■	H	M	T	R	B	D	W	Y	I	E	B	W
W	Q	D	A	I	J	J	C	S	V	U	U	E	E	W
T	O	E	X	P	J	O	A	N	R	V	F	W	E	G
■	O	W	F	R	U	K	C	O	G	J	N	C	T	A
E	H	W	■	H	Y	P	S	J	Q	I	M	O	Q	R
Q	I	O	L	I	R	Y	P	S	Y	F	E	F	Q	N
U	Z	A	U	E	W	C	W	S	S	F	S	Q	W	T
■	A	I	D	R	O	W	O	L	■	Q	E	W	U	G
T	X	F	N	X	A	L	D	■	T	E	S	W	T	K
E	L	D	H	I	R	O	Z	V	F	G	O	Y	Q	I
U	G	Q	F	R	S	T	C	R	M	O	Z	W	O	B
A	G	Y	L	S	L	W	U	A	G	W	U	H	G	C
S	I	V	B	U	Q	E	B	R	I	H	N	S	M	A
A	Q	X	I	B	B	P	C	R	O	S	■	N	S	M
O	B	K	B	L	E	W	Q	D	R	Z	K	E	T	A

G7100029

1. Large sea mammal _ _ _ _ _
2. Floaties _ _ _ _ _ _ _ _ _ _
3. Inquiries _ _ _ _ _ _ _ _ _
4. Females _ _ _ _ _ _
5. LPGA golfer Annika _ _ _ _ _ _ _ _ _
6. Belly **S T O M A C H**
7. One of four sections _ _ _ _ _ _ _ _
8. For riding waves _ _ _ _ _ _ _ _
9. A Guinness book _ _ _ _ _ _ _ _ _ _ _
10. Bush's VP _ _ _ _ _ _ _
11. Firmly twisted wool _ _ _ _ _ _ _
12. Popular in wedding rings _ _ _ _ _ _ _ _ _
13. To splash or stir _ _ _ _ _ _
14. 25 cents _ _ _ _ _ _ _
15. Nelson Mandela's home _ _ _ _ _ _ _ _ _ _ _
16. Canada's "French" province _ _ _ _ _ _ _
Scramble: Machine for winter _ _ _ _ _ _ _ _ _ _

I	F	Z	H	N	Ⓢ	B	A	R	Z	E	P	H	K	L
Q	R	O	E	T	■	E	V	A	W	E	N	U	R	E
R	Z	J	K	Ⓟ	A	U	C	F	T	U	C	A	C	R
E	F	C	R	S	W	B	L	G	A	A	Q	Q	I	D
Z	Ⓟ	S	Y	■	P	S	B	C	C	Ⓢ	M	B	I	■
S	S	T	L	E	E	Ⓜ	E	Z	L	R	N	N	X	E
■	O	R	Ⓢ	M	R	V	O	C	L	H	P	F	Ⓢ	G
P	K	J	V	R	X	N	N	O	Ⓢ	B	M	O	T	H
X	A	M	W	E	K	B	U	T	R	J	O	Ⓜ	O	I
X	P	V	F	Ⓢ	Y	E	M		Ⓢ	G	Ⓟ	N	Ⓞ	M
O	I	F	V	V	I	E	R	I	Q	N	Ⓢ	P	V	D
	N	T	O	Ⓟ	L	T	■	V	A	S	U	E	J	E
	E	Q	N	I	W	B	N	R	■	E	H	Ⓐ	F	Ⓛ
A	H	J	F	K	G	Ⓟ	O	C	Ⓜ	■	W	Ⓡ	C	G
T	I	E	C	T	G	Y	X	O	A	Ⓜ	O	D	Ⓟ	Ⓤ

A4000019

1. 15", 17", 24", for example _ _ _ _ _ _ _ _
2. A business slideshow _ _ _ _ _ _ _ _ _ _ _ _
3. They make the screen tangible _ _ _ _ _ _ _ _ _ _
4. Used to weed out bad emails _ _ _ _ _ _ _ _ _ _ _ _
5. The act of keeping all your work _ _ _ _ _ _ _ _
6. Houses a computer's circuits _ _ _ _ _ _ _ _ _ _ _ _
7. The CPU _ _ _ _ _ _ _ _ _ _
8. Purge, delete and empty the trash _ _ _ _ _ _ _ _ _
9. Right-click _ _ _ _ _ _
10. Programs _ _ _ _ _ _ _ _ _
11. When everybody has to have one **P O P U L A R**
12. A virtue watching the hour glass _ _ _ _ _ _ _ _ _
13. Your set-up _ _ _ _ _ _ _
14. Computers don't lose this, but they run out of it _ _ _ _ _ _ _
15. Measured in GHz _ _ _ _ _ _
16. Not complex _ _ _ _ _ _ _
17. Method of connecting printers before USB _ _ _ _ _ _ _ _ _ _ _ _
Scramble: Used to store and deliver data _ _ _ _ _

I	(T)	O	E	E	■	G	N	(S)	■	O	(H)	O	H	H
N	F	M	B	G	P	B	I	(P)	(U)	(D)	(C)	(Q)	(P)	(A)
I	V	N	U	■	P	W	I	L	D	F	N	J	A	(D)
M	U	I	U	A	A	L	V	E	A	T	Z	T	(T)	(E)
F	(Q)	R	F	Y	I	T	Z	■	(T)	S	T	O	(H)	O
U	C	H	T	Z	L	M	V	E	A	C	H	Z	C	G
B	O	Q	O	C	E	S	(S)	(C)	L	C	C	A	B	G
O	(C)	S	Y	T	■	G	K	A	L	C	E	(H)	K	G
Y	P	M	X	E	(S)	U	■	R	S	K	A	D	N	V
T	W	I	A	F	L	■	N	O	A	X	L	E	R	W
E	E	■	U	N	I	(T)	P	O	T	E	P	K	J	T
X	E	(T)	E	H	(H)	E	F	J	M	A	N	R	■	C
L	D	(S)	■	G	M	O	R	(H)	M	T	F	M	U	Y
T	B	O	H	(C)	A	Y	(S)	S	M	G	T	G	X	I
E	A	P	I	J	N	L	O	I	P	Q	W	E	R	E

A4000009

1. Helps drinks keep their heat _ _ _ _ _ _ _ _ _ _
2. To gauge whether it's iced or hot _ _ _ _ _ _ _ _ _ _ _ _ _
3. Seasonings of tea _ _ _ _ _ _ _ _ _ _ _
4. Usually short and stout _ _ _ _ _ _ _
5. Brand found in a popular coffee chain _ _ _ _ _ _ _ _
6. A tea sans caffeine _ _ _ _ _ _
7. Why coffee shops invented the "sleeve" _ _ _ _ _ _ _ _ _ _ _ _
8. Healing, organic and therapeutic _ _ _ _ _ _ _ _ _
9. Tea's a staple in this large country _ _ _ _ _ _
10. A fancy stir stick _ _ _ _ _ _
11. A flavor with a bear mascot _ _ _ _ _ _ _ _ _ _ _
12. A tea alternative _ _ _ _ _ _ _ _
13. Used instead of hands **T E A C U P S**
14. One lump or two _ _ _ _ _ _
15. Some believe tea can have these powers _ _ _ _ _ _ _ _
16. A way to drink hot tea _ _ _ _ _ _ _ _
17. Tea and coffee do this to your smile _ _ _ _ _ _ _ _ _ _ _ _
Scramble: Common name for several daisy-like plants _ _ _ _ _ _ _ _ _ _

Difficulty: ★★★☆☆

A	G	M	V	X	U	A	Ⓤ	G	N	R	H	E	E	T
G	L	Z	L	Ⓧ	X	X	Ⓢ	Ⓐ	L	A	F	B	J	F
T	R	E	V	S	E	Ⓒ	H	K	V	O	X	Ⓧ	D	Z
O	Z	Ⓝ	E	Q	U	R	Ⓣ	P	U	U	Ⓨ	S	I	A
R	J	O	Ⓤ	A	M	W	I	K	J	U	T	F	K	■
M	J	H	U	Q	A	Z	Q	Ⓝ	U	E	B	R	T	O
B	E	M	O	D	O	N	Q	■	U	Y	E	D	Ⓝ	W
A	C	J	R	Y	S	■	D	Ⓒ	X	A	F	A	X	C
R	T	M	V	X	G	L	D	G	E	P	M	M	X	C
W	E	I	■	S	B	I	R	G	T	A	R	C	E	G
E	Z	Q	P	W	W	N	B	T	J	A	O	Ⓒ	U	D
T	M	E	V	N	Y	J	I	C	S	H	N	K	G	E
Ⓤ	V	Ⓧ	R	L	H	E	Ⓒ	P	F	U	O	F	P	T
U	X	Y	Ⓝ	Y	I	Y	A	E	G	Y	C	U	G	M
C	L	C	P	E	N	■	T	R	Ⓤ	K	N	O	A	L

G7100045

1. Not revised; rough _ _ _ _ _ _ _ _ _
2. Graduating with honors _ _ _ _ _ _ _ _ _
3. A spoon or fork _ _ _ _ _ _ _ _ _
4. Paris' lady _ _ _ _ _ _ _ _ _ _
5. The brains of cells _ _ _ _ _ _ _
6. Carlsbad, Moaning, or Mammoth _ _ _ _ _ _
7. ESPN extreme competition _ _ _ _ _ _ _
8. Haggled, bargained _ _ _ _ _ _ _ _ _
9. The sky's Great Bear _ _ _ _ _ _ _ _ _ _
10. Not sure _ _ _ _ _ _ _ _ _ _
11. Enjoy tents, fires, and nature _ _ _ _ _ _ _
12. Midwestern utility company _ _ _ _ _ _ _ _ _ _
13. A boa _ _ _ _ _ _ _ _ _ _
14. Offensive, disgusting **N A S T Y**
15. The Document Company _ _ _ _ _
Scramble: Unknown influence _ _ _ _ _ _ _ _

Difficulty: ★★⯪☆☆

L	R	M	A	R	■	E	K	C	A	■	L	A	M	N
A	O	G	X	S	A	G	O	R	B	E	F	U	S	I
E	G	B	D	K	R	Q	A	Ⓢ	W	E	D	M	T	W
Z	O	N	Z	Z	N	E	F	Ⓢ	E	■	S	I	Y	F
Y	I	Y	Q	C	I	R	X	■	L	L	R	T	R	I
X	Ⓡ	Q	E	H	T	M	V	A	A	J	U	U	J	S
M	P	I	W	V	H	A	Ⓚ	Ⓚ	N	E	E	D	J	L
Ⓡ	P	P	P	E	■	N	H	D	O	A	K	B	J	Ⓚ
S	E	N	M	T	Ⓡ	A	O	Y	H	Z	T	G	X	Y
T	B	A	N	V	J	P	U	Ⓢ	F	D	F	C	M	O
N	T	C	W	Y	A	N	W	O	E	M	W	A	Ⓚ	N
Q	Ⓐ	Ⓒ	A	D	Ⓢ	D	R	E	I	R	Ⓒ	I	U	R
O	P	Ⓒ	■	A	I	F	N	N	A	X	L	T	E	V
Ⓔ	Y	Ⓘ	H	Ⓒ	S	G	J	V	Y	G	U	I	L	W
S	Ⓡ	Ⓡ	R	Q	I	L	U	B	Ⓡ	O	Y	L	R	E

G7000023

1. Practice before a performance _ _ _ _ _ _ _ _ _ _
2. Rocker Daughtry _ _ _ _ _ _
3. The host _ _ _ _ _ _ _ _ _
4. Not the winner _ _ _ _ _ _ _ _ _
5. Winner over Adam Lambert _ _ _ _ _ _ _ _ _ _
6. Leader of the band _ _ _ _ _ _ _ _ _ _ _ _
7. Took second to Taylor Hicks _ _ _ _ _ _ _ _ _ _ _
8. Before the final round _ _ _ _ _ _ _ _ _ _ _ _
9. Singing the hits at home _ _ _ _ _ _ _ _
10. Composer _ _ _ _ _ _ _ _ _
11. Season 6's polarizing Malakar _ _ _ _ _ _ _ _
12. Along with Kelly, a huge Idol success <u>C</u> <u>A</u> <u>R</u> <u>R</u> <u>I</u> <u>E</u>
13. It's all good, Dog _ _ _ _ _ _
14. Site of the finales for the first 6 seasons _ _ _ _ _ _ _ _ _ _ _ _ _ _
15. An Idol wannabe _ _ _ _ _ _ _ _ _ _ _
16. Hair product sponsor for the show _ _ _ _ _ _ _
Scramble: Sometimes Brutal _ _ _ _ _ _ _ _ _ _ _

L	P	E	R	I	G	C	E	E	D	L	B	L	N	I
H	B	D	F	T	I	U	S	B	I	H	N	B	V	D
A	S	J	L	G	J	B	(H)	K	C	C	M	O	A	H
I	A	A	M	E	W	G	■	T	O	I	O	I	E	L
D	Y	N	(T)	Q	P	L	N	W	C	A	C	T	R	■
B	D	■	G	(T)	K	S	X	B	L	A	M	■	B	M
M	B	T	Y	E	(S)	W	X	I	K	K	H	(H)	(T)	W
D	O	T	E	A	Z	R	D	T	A	Y	E	L	G	F
S	O	V	M	S	R	I	■	D	O	E	(S)	E	Q	T
F	(T)	■	E	E	M	Z	R	K	R	H	Q	O	H	U
A	C	H	K	P	Y	M	X	O	C	V	N	(H)	(A)	I
H	V	U	G	U	Z	(T)	I	S	F	A	D	(E)	J	(N)
M	C	A	Y	L	H	(S)	S	(H)	A	I	(I)	Q	T	H
A	G	P	N	Z	C	Y	N	U	X	J	S	U	T	(S)
O	A	U	U	L	E	N	A	R	(I)	U	N	(P)	(P)	L

G7100014

1. Occurs, takes place **H A P P E N S**
2. Sofa sleeper _ _ _ _ _ _ _ _
3. Risk transfer _ _ _ _ _ _ _ _ _ _
4. Stan Lee's web-slinger _ _ _ _ _ _ _ _ _ _
5. To show appreciation _ _ _ _ _
6. Something preferred or picked _ _ _ _ _ _ _ _ _ _
7. A girl who slept in a walnut shell _ _ _ _ _ _ _ _ _ _ _
8. A Beatle, a Ford, and a President _ _ _ _ _ _ _ _
9. Small prawns _ _ _ _ _ _
10. A sauce of butter, eggs, and lemon juice _ _ _ _ _ _ _ _ _ _ _ _
11. Ruxpin and Paddington _ _ _ _ _ _ _ _ _
12. Home to Florida State _ _ _ _ _ _ _ _ _ _ _
13. Capital of Honduras _ _ _ _ _ _ _ _ _ _ _
14. Producer of one-third of the potatoes in the US _ _ _ _ _
Scramble: Peoria and Champaign _ _ _ _ _ _ _ _

S	A	G	O	D	T	I	J	N	S	N	P	B	C
L	F	S	G	P	Q	M	H	G	L	V	C	C	H	N
S	K	E	C	I	W	P	Y		S	M	Y	J	E	K
U	L	G	R	A	O	F	H	H	N	H	I	D	K	A
S	R	G		E	P	M	F	X	G	B		G	E	R
R	B	T	G	D	N	X	T	P		H	D	D	H	I
E	D	G	W	O	U	P	Q	G	P	J	I	N	A	D
S	O	V	S	H	I	R	F	A	R	I	J	D	N	N
Y	W	M	R	C	T	A	L		E	A	Q	H	A	T
M	O	I	C	U	S	S	C	W	X	R	T	A	F	P
N	P	A	I	Y	A	N	U	E	F		O	D	A	I
P	N	N	A	E	D	I	D	I	K	R	N	A	X	R
Q	A	V	Z	L	U	M	G	P	H	E		L	T	E
O	B	P	F	R	M	V	C	A		E	X	S	Z	E
T	R	E	R	S	Z	H	R	E	P	R	L	S	T	N

A4000014

1. Wedding day to the bride _ _ _ _ _ _ _ _
2. The soon-to-be husband _ _ _ _ _ _
3. Plated or buffet? **D I N N E R**
4. The wedding must go on . . . _ _ _ _ _ _ _ _ _ _ _
5. An embarrassing moment _ _ _ _ _ _
6. A very important expense for the wedding _ _ _ _ _ _ _ _ _ _
7. Courting _ _ _ _ _ _ _
8. The dinner before the wedding day _ _ _ _ _ _ _ _ _ _
9. Usually done prior to an engagement _ _ _ _ _ _ _ _ _ _ _ _ _ _
10. A wonderful help with the wedding! _ _ _ _ _ _ _ _
11. Your store gift list _ _ _ _ _ _ _ _ _
12. Gifts _ _ _ _ _ _ _ _ _
13. Say No to YMCA or the Electric Slide _ _ _ _ _ _ _ _
14. For the champagne _ _ _ _ _ _ _ _
15. Couples reward after the big day _ _ _ _ _ _ _ _ _ _
16. What every bride should feel like on her wedding day _ _ _ _ _ _ _ _
Scramble: A long one's expensive! _ _ _ _ _ _ _ _

I	F	O	E	H	O	L	U	P	■	R	I	W	A	R
T	B	B	C	I	A	Q	B	D	D	W	B	X	S	K
M	S	K	S	B	H	E	R	M	G	C	N	O	K	K
A	C	F	J	D	L	O	M	Y	Y	C	R	Z	Z	E
■	H	N	E	S	I	M	L	U	S	P	E	X	C	V
G	C	H	A	M	J	O	A	L	K	■	E	N	L	U
E	R	■	N	A	C	R	K	Q	D	A	D	Y	W	M
E	N	■	A	X	Z	E	K	I	U	W	K	■	M	■
L	J	U	Z	S	E	T	U	A	I	K	F	T	M	E
Z	V	I	M	U	R	N	B	E	K	A	I	Y	K	K
T	O	R	O	X	X	P	N	M	C	L	T	K	X	D
O	X	E	■	T	J	H	S	O	D	M	U	R	F	N
C	Q	H	I	R	O	P	A	Y	V	E	P	L	L	■
P	L	O	C	X	F	J	Q	I	L	N	P	P	C	A
R	E	M	S	T	Q	E	E	V	A	S	O	B	I	G

G7100011

1. A public vote _ _ _ _ _ _ _ _ _
2. Physical activity _ _ _ _ _ _ _ _ _
3. Capital of the Arab League's most developed country _ _ _ _ _ _ _ _ _ _ _ _ _ _
4. Romania and Ukraine's neighbor _ _ _ _ _ _ _ _
5. Malaysia's capital _ _ _ _ _ _ _ _ _ _ _ _
6. Part of the platonics solids _ _ _ _ _ _ _ _
7. Overly controlling bosses _ _ _ _ _ _ _ _ _ _ _ _ _
8. Center of Australia's Victorian gold rush _ _ _ _ _ _ _ _ _ _
9. Do-over golf shots _ _ _ _ _ _ _ _
10. Time for Easter and blooming flowers E V E R Y S P R I N G
11. Poland's capital before Warsaw _ _ _ _ _ _ _
12. Known for long distance runners and wildlife reserves _ _ _ _ _ _
13. Bodily weaknesses, illnesses _ _ _ _ _ _ _ _ _
14. Medical procedure or educational testing score _ _ _ _ _ _ _ _ _ _ _
15. Atmosphere, surroundings _ _ _ _ _ _ _ _ _ _ _ _
Scramble: World's largest lizard _ _ _ _ _ _ _

G	U	Z	G	G	C	G	T	U	O	P	P	M	M	S
O	F	A	O	U	S	Y	G	V	G	A	E	J	K	Q
R	N	E	O	L	J	J	S	R	H	N	Y	I	H	W
A	V	S	L	C	I	G	R	O	T	V		S	I	E
D	Y	A	L	G	B	B	I	H	T	R	O	P	X	O
A	Y	L	E	C	B	P	R	Q	E	H	H	G	N	B
A	M	N	U	I	G	X	S	A	K	F	N	L	K	O
J	O	G	D	I	A	S		N	L	M	D		K	R
V		H	G	G	O	A	S	W	K	O	P	D	E	C
H	R	F	M	O	M	R	P	D	T	R	O	P	N	O
	K	C	S	Q	P	L	R	A	A	T		M	N	A
E	Z	R		H	U	B	S	E	G	T	N	E	P	G
W	I	Z	O	A	I	M	P	M	Q	I	E	R	N	S
G	D	U	X	Y	R		H	G	Y	N	H	I	L	L
N	T	F	W	M	W	H	A		A	T	H	P	K	U

A4000025

1. The coming together of friends and family _ _ _ _ _ _ _ _ _ _
2. Miniature appetizer burgers _ _ _ _ _ _ _ _
3. The other white meat _ _ _ _ _ _ _ _ _ _
4. Stringy pig _ _ _ _ _ _ _ _ _ _ _
5. To chill with friends _ _ _ _ _ _ _ _
6. An awaited moment on Sundays in fall _ _ _ _ _ _ _ _ _ _
7. Potato, Jell-O, lettuce, or fruit _ _ _ _ _ _
8. Where most grills reside _ _ _ _ _ _
9. Common phrase for heat and touch _ _ _ _ _ _ _ _ _ _ _ _
10. May need a napkin! _ _ _ _ _ _ _
11. Popular side dish for burgers _ _ _ _ _ _ _ _ _ _ _ _
12. The grill's favorite item _ _ _ _ _ _ _ _ _ _
13. No lighter fluid needed! G A S G R I L L
14. Cheap drinks at the bar _ _ _ _ _ _ _ _ _ _
15. Cooling off from the summertime heat _ _ _ _ _ _ _ _ _ _ _ _ _
Scramble: They make for tasty BBQs _ _ _ _ _ _ _ _ _ _

I	K	L	R	A	E	D	■	T	U	E	X	R	I	N
M	S	D	S	S	Y	U	M	O	A	U	F	Z	V	N
E	R	F	Q	W	X	■	Y	A	F	M	Ⓖ	Ⓐ	T	F
Z	G	M	X	Z	R	I	E	T	Y	H	R	L	I	O
H	V	Ⓖ	V	I	W	B	U	■	N	H	B	K	R	M
G	E	J	A	W	W	V	G	S	L	Ⓐ	T	S	R	A
I	Ⓖ	H	D	N	C	E	Ⓖ	Q	H	R	Ⓖ	P	B	U
A	G	N	■	B	A	E	S	T	O	Ⓞ	Ⓐ	Ⓛ	S
J	J	H	M	G	I	U	R	I	L	Ⓞ	T		Z
W	S	Ⓐ	Ⓐ	U	Z	R	K	F	U	W	Z	L	V	N
O	P	V	■	R	E	E	H	E	Ⓐ	Ⓘ	J	M	P	Ⓢ
B	Z	O	Ⓞ	R	Ⓖ	R	E	N	■	Ⓕ	N	G	Ⓓ	Ⓗ
E	I	G	S	A	S	D	O	R	F	R	Q	P	S	■
R	G	H	A	F	T	X	C	A	Ⓞ	L	N	A	H	O
O	N	T	K	E	S	F	F	O	F	E	V	O	■	T

G7100024

1. To assemble or collect _ _ _ _ _ _ _
2. Loved Lancelot _ _ _ _ _ _ _ _ _ _
3. Gagarin or Shepard, for example _ _ _ _ _ _ _ _ _ _
4. Misfired, botched _ _ _ _ _ _ _ _ _
5. Admits, confesses _ _ _ _ _ _ _ _ _ _
6. Cleanser, deodorizer _ _ _ _ _ _ _ _ _ _ _ _ _
7. Popular cracker G O L D F I S H
8. Gleamed, flickered _ _ _ _ _ _ _ _ _ _
9. The English-speaking world's oldest university _ _ _ _ _ _ _
10. Baku is the capital of this country _ _ _ _ _ _ _ _ _ _
11. Munich's sixteen day festival _ _ _ _ _ _ _ _ _ _ _ _ _
12. James Bond's car of choice _ _ _ _ _ _ _ _ _ _ _ _ _ _
13. Wheat or barley, for example _ _ _ _ _ _
14. Acknowledges, admits _ _ _ _ _ _
15. The stomach of birds _ _ _ _ _ _ _
Scramble: Foreign _ _ _ _ _ _ _ _

O	O	V	T	P	B	O	Y	N	G	L	J	E	O	B
I	Q	D	(F)	H	N	L	E	Q	K	W	S	W	M	H
O	H	U	Y	S	H	G	(F)	Z	D	B	F	I	X	F
M	L	E	G	(F)	N	Z	B	U	B	R	D	R	R	S
K	M	B	(F)	(F)	C	I	H	P	L	D	I	A	C	A
R	O	F	G	S	C	B	U	I	G	D	Z	█	E	T
N	I	C	B	N	T	P	B	O	O	B	J	(B)	(B)	E
G	O	A	R	I	E	E	O	V	C	K	L	L	N	M
█	R	F	O	T	B	A	F	A	G	R	(B)	I	N	F
S	U	F	Z	K	N	F	N	A	I	L	E	L	A	T
K	K	L	G	A	Q	L	J	A	G	T	G	S	F	I
J	R	(B)	W	E	T	█	G	C	T	W	T	T	S	X
A	K	D	D	L	P	(B)	(B)	P	G	X	A	(G)	(F)	(F)
N	S	C	Q	A	O	V	R	E	V	P	E	(N)	(N)	(I)
D	A	O	Y	W	W	█	H	T	(F)	Y	R	█	(L)	(Y)

G7000005

1. Robin Hood's skill _ _ _ _ _ _ _ _ _ _ _ _
2. Home of year round golfing and orange groves _ _ _ _ _ _ _ _
3. A gentleman's parlor game _ _ _ _ _ _ _ _ _ _
4. Very high angled golf shot when little green is available _ _ _ _ _ _ _ _ _
5. Dr. James Naismith's game _ _ _ _ _ _ _ _ _ _ _
6. Foul shot _ _ _ _ _ _ _ _ _
7. Violent combat _ _ _ _ _ _ _ _ _
8. A practice begun by the Wrights <u>F</u> <u>L</u> <u>Y</u> <u>I</u> <u>N</u> <u>G</u>
9. A cross between the NHL and lacrosse _ _ _ _ _ _ _ _ _ _ _ _ _
10. A flying disk _ _ _ _ _ _ _ _
11. The weapons of choice for boxers _ _ _ _ _ _
12. An alternative to snow skiing _ _ _ _ _ _ _ _ _
13. A netted enclosure for hitting practice _ _ _ _ _ _ _ _ _ _ _ _
14. Home for an MLB hitter _ _ _ _ _ _ _ _ _ _
Scramble: Rugby, soccer, and gridiron _ _ _ _ _ _ _ _ _

Difficulty: ★★★☆☆

L	D	█	A	H	P	O	B	R	A	H	T	I	P	W
C	V	Y	L	M	V	C	P	M	C	R	T	Q	O	Ⓜ
A	X	D	W	F	K	T	A	█	R	H	U	D	E	W
T	L	Ⓞ	O	O	M	B	Z	O	O	G	I	C	D	O
R	A	S	█	S	H	F	R	U	Q	I	E	L	█	Ⓡ
A	M	Y	N	Z	U	C	C	Ⓞ	C	W	O	X	Ⓜ	J
R	F	Ⓞ	U	R	I	S	J	Ⓞ	N	G	L	K	E	Ⓔ
G	T	N	D	E	H	Ⓣ	O	D	T	Ⓣ	Ⓐ	S	G	Ⓝ
A	N	U	D	█	R	M	Ⓞ	U	D	O	Q	U	C	Ⓣ
█	Ⓜ	A	O	N	O	Y	F	E	Z	S	U	A	G	E
U	J	F	G	T	N	P	B	A	K	X	Ⓔ	B	Ⓜ	N
V	B	A	E	A	E	L	Ⓞ	█	J	H	Y	I	A	L
T	Y	V	G	A	Q	J	C	Ⓜ	Y	S	█	M	G	P
C	M	M	S	I	M	W	B	A	A	Ⓜ	O	D	O	A
S	H	C	Ⓣ	G	Z	A	R	N	C	X	K	E	N	I

G7100003

1. A cloudburst or downpour _ _ _ _ _ _ _ _ _ _ _ _ _
2. Mercedes' more luxurious brother _ _ _ _ _ _ _
3. Homer's epic _ _ _ _ _ _ _ _
4. Capital of Honduras _ _ _ _ _ _ _ _ _ _ _ _
5. Christmas tree accessory _ _ _ _ _ _ _ _ _ _
6. Collective play in sports _ _ _ _ _ _ _ _
7. Tropical "Devilfish" _ _ _ _ _ _ _ _ _ _
8. Smells _ _ _ _ _ _
9. A person who supplies a transplant _ _ _ _ _ _ _ _ _ _ _
10. Historical northern Greece _ _ _ _ _ _ _ _ _ _
11. More hostile, rude **M E A N E R**
12. Cancer or Capricorn _ _ _ _ _ _
13. A very small particle _ _ _ _ _ _ _ _
14. Restraint _ _ _ _ _ _ _ _ _ _
15. A wise female _ _ _ _ _ _ _
16. A worker for Willy Wonka _ _ _ _ _ _ _ _ _ _ _
Scramble: Nicklaus' rival _ _ _ _ _ _ _ _ _

P	C	O	A	D	S	S	■	I	N	■	T	A	F	T
N	Z	U	X	D	A	Y	W	B	Y	O	K	K	N	S
O	I	B	C	■	R	D	R	R	U	E	M	A	D	C
E	H	E	C	T	T	U	O	M	U	R	E	L	Q	E
R	C	I	E	C	U	U	W	M	D	I	R	U	O	M
G	G	O	P	F	L	A	F	D	O	V	J	K	E	M
M	O	Q	R	V	F	K	U	N	Y	T	N	S	L	R
P	S	R	M	A	I	U	Z	X	■	E	O	Q	H	R
T	A	A	P	L	F	■	D	E	R	M	F	B	J	F
E	G	R	T	B	U	■	K	C	X	T	X	B	M	A
L	L	V	I	E	R	M	T	O	E	I	W	T	C	E
I	R	C	U	V	F	O	J	G	N	A	H	M	E	Y
O	M	C	■	S	E	U	L	C	W	R	W	B	K	C
T	F	I	W	S	S	J	S	E	L	F	N	H	P	C
R	E	D	A	F	P	R	C	R	E	Z	X	Y	E	T

BB000008

1. An agreement to buy goods at a later date _ _ _ _ _ _ _
2. Pool of securities _ _ _ _ _ _ _ _ _ _
3. Oil, cotton, beef, grain _ _ _ _ _ _ _ _ _
4. Yearly percentage realized on your investment _ _ _ _ _ _ _ _ _ _ _ _ _ _
5. Future obligation to buy or sell currency at a set price _ _ _ _ _ _ _ _ _ _
6. Used to finance roads, schools, and bridges _ _ _ _ _ _ _ _
7. Buy now, pay later **C R E D I T**
8. CDs, commercial paper, T-Bills _ _ _ _ _ _ _ _ _ _ _
9. Difference between bid and ask prices _ _ _ _ _ _
10. Dollar, Yen, Euro _ _ _ _ _ _ _ _
11. The rate does not change _ _ _ _ _
12. Assets used to secure a loan _ _ _ _ _ _ _ _ _ _
13. Exchanging of securities for one another _ _ _ _ _
14. Ownership in a company _ _ _ _ _
15. Land and buildings _ _ _ _ _ _ _ _ _ _
16. Issued by a company to finance debt _ _ _ _ _ _ _ _ _ _ _ _ _ _
Scramble: Buy now, but agree to sell later _ _ _ _ _ _ _ _ _ _ _

Difficulty: ★★★☆☆

B	A	O	M	O	E	V	M	L	T	A	Z	O	U	N
E	Y	U	Y	A	P	L	C	O	P	F	K	E	U	O
■	H	U	A	Y	H	I	O	O	W	K	E	W	U	L
H	P	C	Y	C	M	Q	F	E	B	P	T	F	M	T
E	E	W	D	■	J	I	S	E	O	H	E	R	T	A
M	T	■	A	N	I	A	V	T	E	G	H	J	I	T
I	Q	C	K	P	A	G	D	C	W	F	I	S	H	O
P	A	E	D	I	M	J	W	A	C	E	G	A	D	N
H	X	B	I	O	Z	S	G	T	G	Z	X	W	B	O
J	I	I	S	A	O	L	P	V	T	N	L	R	U	C
C	V	Z	X	T	X	H	T	T	E	N	D	Q	K	O
A	M	R	P	U	O	L	L	H	C	F	R	A	Q	C
B	S	K	N	M	T	R	R	C	R	B	Z	G	M	Y
Y	U	O	X	K	U	X	C	O	K	F	P	C	E	T
N	A	O	T	G	H	O	A	T	U	T	■	D	I	E

G7100018

1. Covered, grassy **C A R P E T E D**
2. Trachea _ _ _ _ _ _
3. One hump or two _ _ _ _ _ _
4. 100 runs in cricket _ _ _ _ _ _ _ _
5. A Turkish nut used in praline _ _ _ _ _ _ _ _ _
6. Animal stuffer _ _ _ _ _ _ _ _ _ _ _
7. Nicaragua's northern neighbor _ _ _ _ _ _ _ _ _
8. 1994 figure skating Olympic Champion _ _ _ _ _ _ _
9. A short musical drama _ _ _ _ _ _ _ _ _
10. La Dolce Vita _ _ _ _ _ _ _ _ _ _ _ _
11. Deduction, idea _ _ _ _ _ _ _ _
12. Rival of Nicklaus _ _ _ _ _ _ _ _ _ _
13. Titmouse _ _ _ _ _ _ _ _ _ _
14. Final objectives for base runners _ _ _ _ _ _ _ _ _ _ _ _
15. D-Day's destination _ _ _ _ _ _ _ _ _ _ _
Scramble: Footstool _ _ _ _ _ _ _ _

S	J	I	A	T	G	Q	R	R	W	Y	D	X	U	E
A	I	X	L	J		U	O	T	E	R	B	J	I	M
L	E	T	T	I	I	B	D	O	M	C	U	H	C	I
K	O	K	S	D	F	K	G	V	T	Z	M	M	A	P
G	H	N	R	H	R	P	H	B	Z	T	N	D	A	N
T	R	W	G	I	A	S	E	B	G	O	X	F	G	S
K	C	W	A	G	L	O	D	X	H	P	L	M	T	X
O	G	W	Z	I	J	Q	W	E	G	R	V	S	O	N
K	A	N	A	T	F	L	F	S	N	V	O	S	P	
Q	R	H	G	G	E	A	D	P	G	E	G	F	E	E
N	A	N	U	U	Y	A	R	B	D	E	T	I	Q	S
	R	Y	T	S	G	E		S	C	E	S	R	O	E
I	W	E	O	N	Z	K	E	Y		H	S	A	J	W
E	Z	T	L	Y	Q	T	C	L	S	C	V	Y	O	V
A	M	K	R	E	U	G	P	R		G	A	L	T	A

A4000015

1. A bike for two _ _ _ _ _ _
2. Be careful of this around corners _ _ _ _ _
3. A term for the frame design _ _ _ _ _ _ _ _
4. Helpful when climbing a hill _ _ _ _ _ _ _ _ _ _
5. Riding in place _ _ _ _ _ _ _ _ _ _
6. Skinny or fat _ _ _ _ _ _
7. Italy's Tour _ _ _ _ _ _ _ _ _ _
8. A large pack of riders _ _ _ _ _ _ _ _ _
9. Escape the city **G E T A W A Y**
10. A worthwhile part of long rides _ _ _ _ _ _ _
11. Required of pros to come out on top _ _ _ _ _ _ _ _ _
12. These can be bad if you crash _ _ _ _ _ _ _
13. Mountain biking trail _ _ _ _ _ _ _ _ _ _ _ _
14. Covering a team jersey _ _ _ _ _ _ _ _ _ _ _
15. Events containing three sports in one _ _ _ _ _ _ _ _ _ _
16. A seat _ _ _ _ _ _ _
Scramble: Mountain terrain rating _ _ _ _ _ _ _ _ _

Difficulty: ★★★☆☆

M	B	A	R	E	W	N	■	B	E	R	J	J	I	T
E	G	G	F	H	V	V	S	O	O	H	T	E	■	G
T	N	Z	D	J	M	R	L	O	F	F	Q	M	K	M
P	J	W	Z	P	O	L	T	C	V	W	I	M	F	H
D	B	J	L	S	M	B	B	B	L	A	A	C	A	S
Q	A	Q	X	Y	O	V	V	U	O	J	O	■	S	I
I	Z	E	S	E	W	R	O	Y	Y	H	Z	R	Y	A
E	M	A	N	O	I	I	C	N	G	J	E	X	P	P
E	I	T	O	Z	P	X	J	C	A	H	A	D	E	D
O	T	O	C	N	X	N	M	K	Z	E	E	L	H	O
R	A	R	E	Y	U	■	K	L	J	L	G	U	K	I
N	K	E	A	A	Z	S	U	A	A	E	V	J	P	N
T	R	G	Z	I	■	N	E	S	S	I	H	P	V	Z
U	K	Q	D	R	S	U	D	J	G	P	W	K	I	T
S	E	V	D	O	U	■	B	L	U	T	C	Y	F	Y

G7100020

1. Rudyard Kipling's anthropomorphic tale _ _ _ _ _ _ _ _ _ _ _ _
2. A German airship _ _ _ _ _ _ _ _ _
3. Alert, watchful _ _ _ _ _ _ _ _ _ _ _
4. Winner of 18 Majors _ _ _ _ _ _ _ _ _ _ _ _
5. North America's first English settlement _ _ _ _ _ _ _ _ _ _ _
6. Clothing fasteners _ _ _ _ _ _ _ _ _
7. May beetles _ _ _ _ _ _ _ _ _
8. Risk seeking, hazardous _ _ _ _ _ _ _ _ _ _ _ _ _
9. Oldest branch of Mathematics _ _ _ _ _ _ _ _ _ _ _ _
10. The Democratic Republic of the Congo's predecessor _ _ _ _ _ _
11. Popular quiz show **J E O P A R D Y**
12. An island in the desert _ _ _ _ _
13. A Fairy Tale's beginning _ _ _ _ _ _ _ _ _ _ _ _ _ _
14. A public speaker _ _ _ _ _ _ _
15. Exercise or an undertaking _ _ _ _ _ _ _ _ _
Scramble: Tropical minnows Danio Rerio _ _ _ _ _ _ _ _ _ _ _

I	S	F	F	L	O	P	I	E	N	A	S	O O	P
L	K	G	T	A	Z	K	T	A	G	F	C	R	A O
I	D	X	H	I	X	Z	C	R	B	Y	F	A	E E
T	T	B	L	E	D	U	H	G	H	B	N		G	U
	M	R	E	R	A	A	C	R	H	W	W	O	E	Z
R	S	G	M	A	I	H		L	E	E	V	K	G	F
V	C	G	X	H	M	J	G	M	R	R	I	M	E	S
V	V	C	D	C	U	S	E	C	B	D	L	J	R	S
E	K	B	B	W	E	G	B	G	H	E	Y	A	P	N
T	S	A	M	O	H	D	S	X	I	R	V	H	M	K
M	K	S	J	G	O	J	G		Q	L	N	P	A	Z
U	Q	C	M	Q	G	E	A	B	S	C	Q	T	E	C
D	E	W	V	J	L	Y	Y	O	A	C	O	H	Q	I
D	N	J	Z	E	I	H	W	R	U	R	X	U	A	O
N	B	I	A	L	A	H	L	T	S	I	C	H	L	L

BB000009

1. Invaded Poland _ _ _ _ _ _ _
2. The world conflict _ _ _ _ _ _ _
3. Those who fled the war _ _ _ _ _ _ _ _ _
4. Anti-submarine weapon developed by the Royal Navy _ _ _ _ _ _ _ _ _ _
5. Prime Minister of Britain _ _ _ _ _ _ _ _ _
6. Eastern Europe's political and economic system after the war _ _ _ _ _ _ _ _ _ _ _
7. Nazi leader _ _ _ _ _ _ _ _ _ _ _ _ _
8. Non-Jewish caucasian race _ _ _ _ _ _
9. Nazi period, German state _ _ _ _ _
10. Led the secret police, Nazi's second in command _ _ _ _ _ _ _ _ _
11. Guides a missile towards its target _ _ _ _ _ _ _ _
12. Famous German naval warship **G R A F S P E E**
13. Conventions that provided rules for humane treatment _ _ _ _ _ _ _
14. Annexed by Nazi's in 1939 _ _ _ _ _ _ _ _
15. Non-cooperation, "The Underground" _ _ _ _ _ _ _ _ _ _
16. Western economic system _ _ _ _ _ _ _ _ _ _ _ _
17. Poisonous showers _ _ _ _ _ _ _ _ _ _ _
Scramble: Standard weapon _ _ _ _ _ _ _ _ _ _ _ _

Difficulty: ★★★☆☆

```
N K A A V L G N T H ▮ N A E R
J E Z L A Z F Q E Q N D K M S
D R Y K F I Y I U W M B I B Q
K C H C U U C T Z E L R L L ▮
U C C C O O S Q A P O R P T ▮
I J U J C U P B D A I E O U N
P U S D K T W J K ▮ B L S O E
M Q Y Q V U R A S Y D N H G I
I T A E T Y A ▮ A T I T E N N
L P W E V L U I G N R U I N R
C A N U A T N N X U H K A U G
▮ D R Q M I Q R K G T L O S G
S E N H I ▮ L A N I K K U F A
E X C E L Y X P N N M B F T E
N S ▮ V V E R N D E Q M R M A
```

G7100030

1. A trap in the desert Q U I C K S A N D
2. Loving, affectionate _ _ _ _ _ _ _ _ _
3. Goal of the Deadliest Catch _ _ _ _ _ _ _ _ _ _
4. One fourth _ _ _ _ _ _ _ _
5. Includes the Horseshoe Falls _ _ _ _ _ _ _ _
6. Burning aromas _ _ _ _ _ _ _ _ _
7. Holland _ _ _ _ _ _ _ _ _ _ _ _ _
8. Singing grasshoppers _ _ _ _ _ _ _ _ _
9. Bush's VP _ _ _ _ _ _ _
10. Emergency dial _ _ _ _ _ _ _ _ _ _ _
11. Peter Pan's world _ _ _ _ _ _ _ _ _ _ _
12. Musical tool _ _ _ _ _ _ _ _ _ _ _
13. Pertaining to the second power in mathematics _ _ _ _ _ _ _ _ _ _
14. Home to the Petronas Twin Towers _ _ _ _ _ _ _ _ _ _ _ _ _
Scramble: Explains _ _ _ _ _ _ _ _ _ _

C	M	T	E	K	A	N	C	K	O	E	A	I	E	E
O	A	Y	P	D	S	C	A	X	O	H	A	K	V	H
I	L	O	Y	R	C	E	J	B	Z	T	S	D	N	B
P	G	E	R	M	Z	G	M	L	V	K	S	C	C	R
R	W	O	C	T	I	M	H	B	U	U	I	Q	Y	M
S	I	B	Q	F	N	B	F	E	I	R	W	I	S	G
V	E	C	C	P	A	Y	C		A	Q	N	G	D	F
E	D	L	O	U	U	E	E	C	E	U	Y	A	Z	D
	R	X	O		O	G	G	D	U	O	Q	L	Z	X
R	G	P	P	C	P	L	B	G	A	D	F	S	R	U
D	R	N	W	M	F	E	D	E	O	A	S	D	I	F
J	E	C	L	I	N	H	E	T	Y	L	O	J	W	Y
A	D	V	J	P	P	C		D	I	Y	C	G	H	P
E	G	D	M	L	I	U	U	C	E	D	X	E	H	T
S	T	H	U	O	S	E	M	R	I	H	E	E	X	O

A4000013

1. A helpful adviser for kicking a habit _ _ _ _ _ _ _ _ _ _ _
2. Maintains a healthy body _ _ _ _ _ _ _ _ _
3. Requires self medicated shots _ _ _ _ _ _ _ _ _
4. All foods have this "intake" _ _ _ _ _ _ _ _
5. Not lethargy _ _ _ _ _ _ _
6. Cleanse _ _ _ _ _ _ _ _ _
7. Symptom of a lung problem, mild or severe _ _ _ _ _ _ _ _ _
8. A conditional seizure _ _ _ _ _ _ _ _ _
9. A PCP **D O C T O R**
10. There's a good kind and bad kind _ _ _ _ _ _ _ _ _ _ _ _ _
11. Cancer causing agent _ _ _ _ _ _ _ _ _ _ _ _
12. Performed annually for prevention _ _ _ _ _ _
13. Required before some employment _ _ _ _ _ _ _ _ _ _ _
14. Atkins, South Beach, etc. _ _ _ _ _ _
15. Usually pretty "common" _ _ _ _ _ _
Scramble: Requires extra oxygen _ _ _ _ _ _ _ _ _

V	T	K	S	I	F	R	(N)	F	E	R	M	A	I	A
K	J	E	(A)	G	G	P	E	S	C	W	J	T	X	W
F	O	U	B	C	U	C	J	L	O	W	A	N	N	G
G	H	L	L	(C)	G	H	M	A	Z	M	V	T	G	R
Q	K	L	(A)	(C)	S	U	N	B	B	I	S	(Y)	P	N
C	I	W	Q	C	Z	A	■	(L)	F	(E)	F	M	I	R
E	B	K	P	V	M	H	E	Y	T	V	Y	M	(N)	X
R	A	N	V	O	O	D	H	(E)	Q	F	X	(R)	H	X
■	N	U	G	B	O	K	P	Y	U	(C)	(C)	E	Z	Z
T	H	K	K	I	Z	M	N	Y	N	L	M	E	U	T
Q	J	S	B	P	G	E	H	O	Y	X	N	C	Y	A
W	A	(N)	E	C	H	■	A	M	W	P	P	A	O	Q
R	K	U	U	B	K	(A)	■	C	I	Y	(A)	D	(A)	(C)
L	Q	U	X	E	A	Z	E	N	B	J	A	N	B	O
O	R	A	H	V	D	N	R	B	(N)	J	A	A	L	M

BB000010

1. Popular South Asian flatbread _ _ _ _ _ _ _ _ _
2. The log portion of "Ants on a Log" **C E L E R Y**
3. Main ingredient in Guacamole _ _ _ _ _ _ _ _
4. Marsala, fried, grilled, buffalo _ _ _ _ _ _ _ _
5. Seedless orange _ _ _ _ _ _ _ _ _ _ _ _
6. A pickle's main ingredient _ _ _ _ _ _ _ _ _
7. Healthy nut _ _ _ _ _ _ _
8. Spice used to flavor cereals and fruits _ _ _ _ _ _ _ _
9. Peaches without fuzz _ _ _ _ _ _ _ _ _ _ _
10. Have hearts and used for a famous dip _ _ _ _ _ _ _ _ _ _ _ _
11. Granny Smith, Gala, Golden Delicious _ _ _ _ _ _
12. Small fruits, often dried, high in potassium _ _ _ _ _ _ _ _ _
13. Kellogg breakfast bar _ _ _ _ _ _ _ _ _ _ _
14. Rough skinned melon _ _ _ _ _ _ _ _ _ _ _
15. Seeds used to make chocolate _ _ _ _ _ _
Scramble: Cultivated for white seeds _ _ _ _ _ _ _ _ _

Difficulty: ★★★☆☆

L	P	P	N	Y	Z	I	E	E	D	E	T	V	U	O
E	V	B	L	D	R	Q	K	W	A	V	D	O	L	O
A	T	H	B	I	P	W	G	B	O	P	J	I	S	O
Y	M	W	D	F	C	E		L	I	C	E	R	R	I
E	J	N	G	A	R	Q	N	Y	H	A	M	E	L	
A	C	Z	L	F	N	W	C	R	W	E	C		A	G
L	T	K	L	E	F	X	M	O	O	V	S	W	G	G
D	Y	I	R	W	E	E	D	Y	T	C	M	I	Z	W
R	K	R	T	U	R	I		N	H	D	G	L	U	M
L	D	G	T	C	V	O	D	M	E	C	K	H	R	E
T	N	S	E	H	J	S	U	N	Q	P	G	D	E	
R	K	M	H	Z	U	D	G	I	H	N	E	E	U	R
H	Y	N	U	O	A	G	I	D	R	N	W	H	W	B
O	P	D	N	V	M	W	L	J	B	S	L	K	F	S
H	E	Q	W	C	A	A	I	S	W	P	I	E	B	

G7100042

1. Speculated, doubted _ _ _ _ _ _ _ _ _
2. Romeo's bard _ _ _ _ _ _ _ _
3. A Diamond is Forever _ _ _ _ _ _ _ _
4. Scooping earth underwater _ _ _ _ _ _ _ _ _
5. Friendly, sociable, outgoing _ _ _ _ _ _ _ _ _ _ _ _
6. To dismantle or dissect _ _ _ _ _ _ _ _ _ _ _ _ _ _
7. Pomegranate syrup _ _ _ _ _ _ _ _ _ _
8. A buzz, hum, or vibration _ _ _ _ _ _
9. Cooperation, compromise _ _ _ _ _ _ _ _ _ _ _ _ _
10. A country working girl _ _ _ _ _ _
11. Window cleaner _ _ _ _ _ _ _
12. Sparkled, flickered _ _ _ _ _ _ _ _ _ _ _ _
13. Flashy, tasteless **G A R I S H**
14. Home to the Greek oracle, Pythia _ _ _ _ _ _ _
15. Tombstone's hero _ _ _ _ _ _ _ _ _ _
Scramble: Composed An American in Paris _ _ _ _ _ _ _ _ _

T	H	(P)	I	P	R	I	B	V	I	V	N	(R)	(U)	T
C	H	A	S	R	D	Z	A	E	F	(U)	O	O	(X)	(L)
K	X	L	V	M	B	S	P	O	M	G	X	X	T	V
I	G	I	T	T	U	V	Y	O	T	G	U	(Y)	S	A
C	R	(T)	I	S	X	F	E	F	P	W	G	N	■	G
(T)	Z	N	I	X	L	F	O	(T)	P	Y	L	P	(P)	J
I	U	M	W	L	K	U	Y	(L)	E	U	A	O	N	N
T	A	D	N	C	L	(A)	N	I	■	(L)	R	D	H	I
E	K	O	N	F	O	T	S	■	S	P	J	I	N	(T)
N	I	E	Q	V	Z	R	Q	H	K	O	H	X	Z	A
T	Z	K	O	S	E	H	J	Y	L	I	I	D	(T)	P
Q	G	I	H	■	N	P	(A)	A	W	(P)	S	K	B	A
H	D	Y	Z	O	H	Q	T	(L)	S	A	■	I	D	C
O	B	T	W	G	I	J	Y	L	D	(A)	N	N	T	E
A	G	N	(P)	R	B	A	I	R	V	B	U	E	U	R

A4000018

1. Eleventh hour deals and getaways _ _ _ _ _ _ _ _ _ _ _
2. Where most travelers convene _ _ _ _ _ _ _ _ _ _ _ _
3. Figuring the trip's agenda _ _ _ _ _ _ _ _ _
4. Excitement, a risky trip _ _ _ _ _ _ _ _ _ _
5. Indicated by a 4 or 5 star L U X U R Y
6. Camping, hotels, etc. _ _ _ _ _ _ _ _
7. Sightseeing, exhausting _ _ _ _ _ _ _ _
8. Delta, Southwest _ _ _ _ _ _ _ _
9. Found at many hot spots and airports _ _ _ _ _
10. Even tips are included! _ _ _ _ _ _ _ _ _ _ _ _ _
11. Re-set your watch _ _ _ _ _ _ _ _ _
12. Only bring what you need _ _ _ _ _ _ _ _ _ _
13. Say "Cheese" _ _ _ _ _ _ _ _ _ _ _ _
14. Found everywhere in NYC and large cities _ _ _ _ _ _ _ _ _
15. For leaving the country _ _ _ _ _ _ _ _ _
16. Keeps you on "track" _ _ _ _ _
Scramble: Excitement before a trip _ _ _ _ _ _ _ _ _ _ _ _ _

Difficulty: ★★★☆☆

```
S Z E T I U U P N V E H Q K I
N O X I D   O R O P P Y S R N
T L C E B E M D S T X M O Q O
F H V P I Z W S J N Z F X I F
T B A S T K W L C S S C B R
  O Q M R T O Y M Q H D K D T
W E F L P R I C U G M T J U C
R Z X J I U S O O P E Z R O N
V A T T H A U T E D J I U P
S M V P U   M I E P V S X T
T E H K J U A N L B O P R K G
M E N G P R M   V A E B O B N
S A P S I G S U U R R F E U L
G G F P L C D M Q E P P Y B P
N C A H   O N L U I U M N A N
```

G7100044

1. Prickly "hedgehog" of the sea _ _ _ _ _ _ _
2. Location of chimneys and shingles _ _ _ _ _ _ _ _ _ _ _
3. An Oriental sword _ _ _ _ _ _ _ _ _
4. Mexican "language" incorporating many American words _ _ _ _ _ _ _ _ _ _
5. To delay _ _ _ _ _ _ _ _ _
6. Hockey's cup _ _ _ _ _ _ _ _
7. Teenage movie rating _ _ _ _ _ _ _ _ _ _ _ _ _ _
8. Extracted, overturned **U P R O O T E D**
9. *Kill Bill*'s Beatrix _ _ _ _ _ _ _ _ _ _ _
10. Nobel psychologist who first described classical conditioning _ _ _ _ _ _ _
11. The ocean's flow after the full moon _ _ _ _ _ _ _ _ _ _ _
12. 1977 Triple Crown winner _ _ _ _ _ _ _ _ _ _ _ _ _
13. A fork's tine _ _ _ _ _ _
14. To experience, sustain _ _ _ _ _ _ _ _
15. Enforcement of the Eighteenth Amendment _ _ _ _ _ _ _ _ _ _ _
16. Earthy, reddish-brown pigment _ _ _ _ _ _
Scramble: Chinese vermilion _ _ _ _ _ _ _

O	C	K	F	A	Ⓛ	V	A	O	G	X	O	G	G	H
C	A	M	W	D	A	C	N	D	M	O	I	F	J	T
R	L	B	H	Ⓑ	A	H	S	R	A	U	C	F	Z	N
T	U	S	A	Y	U	U	W	E	Z	W	J	I	Ⓗ	I
Q	Ⓗ	Ⓛ	Ⓐ	L	B	E	X	N		C	H	E	R	Ⓑ
R	I	Ⓛ	Ⓕ	Ⓐ	Ⓛ	S	O	Q	V	G	J	P	T	
	N	G	Ⓑ	Ⓢ	E	P	L	A	P	J	Z	Ⓛ	A	X
I	O	O	R	G	T	T	V	Z	E	N	P	Ⓛ	M	E
R	M	B	T	E	Q	T	M	W	R		G	W	M	N
D	R	B	J	Ⓑ	Y	I	N		Ⓗ	S	U	G	E	Ⓑ
D		K	I	Q	E	R	K	R	V	I	O	B	X	Ⓗ
O	X	N	E	Ⓑ	B	U	E	R	A	E	C	H	V	S
Ⓗ	M	O	L	E	E	U	H	H	H	Y	H	N	H	A
F	K	R	T	I	A	Q	P	T	A	L	N	F	D	
Y	H	L	D	N	R	E	X	Ⓗ	S	Ⓛ	A	I	L	R

G7000024

1. Steve-O's partner _ _ _ _ _ _
2. Derek and Julianne _ _ _ _ _ _ _
3. Head judge _ _ _ _ _ _ _ _ _ _ _
4. Kristi Yamaguchi and Shawn Johnson's partner **B A L L A S**
5. Female host Samantha _ _ _ _ _ _
6. N'Sync star _ _ _ _ _ _ _ _ _
7. Season 7 winner _ _ _ _ _ _ _ _ _ _
8. A boxer light on his feet _ _ _ _ _ _ _ _ _
9. Celebrity who partnered with Julianne and Edyta _ _ _ _ _ _
10. Ty Murray's professional partner Chelsie _ _ _ _ _ _ _ _ _
11. Blossom star Joey and football star Taylor _ _ _ _ _ _ _ _ _
12. Where host Samantha performed Chicago _ _ _ _ _ _ _ _ _
13. Male host Tom _ _ _ _ _ _ _
14. Season 4 contestant Mills _ _ _ _ _ _ _ _
15. R&B singer Toni _ _ _ _ _ _ _
16. Steve Wozniak pulled this in Season 8 _ _ _ _ _ _ _ _
17. Singer Carlisle _ _ _ _ _ _ _
Scramble: Season 2's Soap star _ _ _ _ _ _ _ _ _

Difficulty: ★★★⯪☆

Y	H	O	O	O	U	D	O	B	E	O	K	W	S	R
I	F	L	O	R	O	Q	H	B	U	D	A	H	O	E
G	V	A	U	V	J	D	M	A	T	M	M	F	I	J
T	C	R	W	P	A	N	N	J	A	M	D	O	V	N
T	T	A	T	X	K	B	J	C	Y	U	E	Y	A	N
N	K	T	R	B	Q	D	X	E	A	X	A	H	I	I
E	S	O	R	D	U	U	H	R	O	Q	S	A	A	Z
M	A	F	E	M	C	D	I	G	P	P	J	N	M	R
L	S	H	A	V	T		A	K	G		M	J	A	G
I	R	N	W	V	A	T	W	S	H	N	Y	A	V	J
A	B	L	B	I	I	H	G	A	Z	U	I	Z	V	A
R	Z	W	D	C	W	C	O	K	Q	Y	N	E	R	N
C	X	X	E	T	P	D	E	L	A	I		V	F	E
Q	O	D	K	C	F	Q	N	I	L	E	F	R	Z	S
N	O	E		T	M	E	M	N	A	V	E	N	O	I

G7100049

1. Completely different _ _ _ _ _ _ _ _ _
2. Ruled by a few _ _ _ _ _ _ _ _ _ _
3. Created Pong and the 2600 _ _ _ _ _ _
4. Bayer's multivitamin line _ _ _ _ _ _ _ _
5. Michael Corleone and Tony Montana _ _ _ _ _ _ _ _ _ _ _ _ _
6. Site of the Nazi Party Conventions _ _ _ _ _ _ _ _ _ _
7. Pertaining to newborns _ _ _ _ _ _ _ _ _
8. A chain of islands _ _ _ _ _ _ _ _ _ _ _ _
9. In contrast to _ _ _ _ _ _ _ _
10. Dignified, Aristocratic _ _ _ _ _ _
11. Great White's third studio album _ _ _ _ _ _ _ _ _ _ _ _
12. Disgust, repulsion _ _ _ _ _ _ _ _ _
13. Bond film *Never Say* . . . _ _ _ _ _ _ _ _ _ _ _ _
14. Verbally reject, oppose _ _ _ _ _ _ _
15. Goldfinger's henchman _ _ _ _ _
16. Enlisted member of the US Air Force A I R M A N
Scramble: German-born leader of Luna Negra _ _ _ _ _ _ _ _ _ _ _ _ _ _

Difficulty: ★★★⯪☆ PUZZLE 85: **Michael Jackson**

N	L	S	O	V	T	M	P	O	D	J	I	I	T	U
O	S	B	H	C	X	K	N	O	D	E	G	G	A	D
S	E	P	J	A	I	F	J	T	Y	N	P	L	T	Z
A	I	M	N	D	M	K	P	U	N	K	A	T	R	I
D	E	D	A	T	C	W	T	D	P	D	R	O	S	T
M	N	W	■	B	I	B	N	S	J	Y	P	Y	J	H
T	Z	V	E	M	A	K	W	N	A	K	S	Z	K	A
D	A	D	■	K	L	S	R	O	R	B	Y	Q	A	V
O	F	D	E	T	D	W	L	■	E	R	B	J	U	U
H	T	V	B	X	I	O	F	C	Q	B	S	S	W	Y
C	Q	S	G	N	■	O	C	L	V	■	G	M	B	O
R	U	E	I	B	A	H	A	B	F	S	I	S	I	E
D	Z	W	V	A	W	I	U	D	P	U	A	Y	B	L
O	V	Q	H	R	A	M	U	U	L	R	G	I	X	L
R	X	W	E	■	M	R	T	S	T	H	O	R	E	L

BB000005

1. Significant event performance in 1993 _ _ _ _ _ _ _ _ _ _ _ _
2. Themes of supernatural and paranoia _ _ _ _ _ _ _ _ _ _
3. His chimp _ _ _ _ _ _ _ _
4. Final Number 1 from "Bad" album _ _ _ _ _ _ _ _ _ _ _
5. Third solo album released in 1973 _ _ _ _ _ _ _ _ _ _ _
6. It doesn't matter who's wrong or right, just . . . _ _ _ _ _ _
7. Duet performed with sister, Janet _ _ _ _ _ _ _
8. Verb often used to describe his physical changes _ _ _ _ _
9. First album to ever have 8 UK Top 20 hits _ _ _ _ _ _ _ _ _ _
10. Signature move _ _ _ _ _ _ _ _
11. Guest starred on the "Stark Raving Dad" episode _ _ _ _ _ _ _ _ _
12. Written with Paul McCartney _ _ _ _ _ _ _ _ _ _ _
13. Jackson 5 guitar player _ _ _ _ _ _ _ _ _ _ _ _ _
14. A generation grew up watching Thriller _ _ _ _ _ _ _ _ _
15. Junkie from HIStory **T A B L O I D**
16. Tragedy in June, 2009 _ _ _ _ _ _
Scramble: Largest grossing tour in history _ _ _ _ _ _ _ _ _ _ _ _ _

Difficulty: ★★★⯪☆

T	G	T	A	L	H	X	D	S	R	R	K	N	O	F
B	O	C	K	Q	A	E	S		E	V	B	C	A	H
O	W	S	I	R	Z	Q	O	P	Z	L	U	T	O	M
O	U	M	I	E	S	D	M	T	X	U	E	D	Z	T
G	U	C	O	Q	Y	J	D		T	H	A	Y	J	H
D	N	I	Q	I	C	R	W	P	D	U	G	O	R	E
Y	U	W	D	G	B	A	W	I	F	W	T	S	Q	E
S	Z	E		E	H	R	R	O	N	U	A	J	P	L
R	D	K	T	V	O	E	D	Y	B	X	W	A	T	J
A	L	U	W	F	H	S	V	P	I	N	F	B	K	C
U	W	S		T	I	E	W	L	N	T	F	Z	V	R
I	K	L	T	W	N	A	O	X	T	S	B	K	E	Y
S	C	T	P	G	A	B	R		A	R	G	P	A	
W	U	A	V	F	S	M	J	U	L	H	Y	H	N	T
L	I	J	A	A	R		E	X	L	R	A	M		S

G7100027

1. Rain's shield **U M B R E L L A**
2. America's personification _ _ _ _ _ _ _ _ _
3. Sleipuir, Pegasus, or a unicorn _ _ _ _ _ _ _ _ _ _ _
4. Upheaval, disorder _ _ _ _ _ _ _
5. Afghanistan, Uzbekistan, and China's neighbor _ _ _ _ _ _ _ _ _ _ _ _ _
6. "Get's" meetings or gatherings _ _ _ _ _ _ _ _ _ _
7. Least populous state _ _ _ _ _ _ _ _ _
8. Poland's capital _ _ _ _ _ _ _ _
9. Customary _ _ _ _ _ _
10. Wall art in a castle _ _ _ _ _ _ _ _ _ _
11. Fried tortilla _ _ _ _ _ _ _ _
12. An MLB team's goal _ _ _ _ _ _ _ _ _ _ _ _ _
13. Site of the PGA's Buick Invitational _ _ _ _ _ _ _ _ _ _ _ _ _
14. Written authorizations _ _ _ _ _ _ _ _ _
15. Location for a home's shingles _ _ _ _ _ _ _ _ _ _ _ _
Scramble: Australia's Pademelon _ _ _ _ _ _ _ _

A	M	R	G	N	L	V	O	S	J	H	A	F	V	R
G	K	I	T	I		G	N	I	F	A	Y	X	N	D
T	J	O	U	B	N	U	E	I	T	Y	P	O	K	L
T	O	C	I	Y	B	C	O	O	I	U	P	E	D	E
U	R	A	S	P	I	L	F	C	Q	L	O	F	B	
Q	E	S		M		L	R	W	C	N	X	Q	P	I
L		F	U	L	E	H	D	Z	N	H	G	F	A	Y
R	S	S	V	E	K	Z	F	A	B	G	J	H	S	H
A	M	X	W	B	Q	H	M	T	E	H	N	F	I	H
H	A	C	C	B	R	E	A	L	W	I	B	B	A	F
J	I	F	C	X	I	I	N	M	S	E	O	F	U	B
I	Y	T	I	L	S	H	G	F	G	E	T	E	K	R
B	Y	L	S	A	N	P	K	V	I	L	L		B	T
K	W	M	D	B	V	G	F	D	L	T	J	A	V	S
C	Z	A	S		G	N	Z	A	L	F	I	C	N	B

BB000003

1. Throwing an artificial lure _ _ _ _ _ _ _ _ _ _ _ _
2. Resembles fish prey _ _ _ _ _ _
3. Some are hand tied _ _ _ _ _ _
4. Used to attract large fish _ _ _ _ _ _ _ _ _
5. Close together line toss, locates feeding fish _ _ _ _ _ _ _ _ _
6. Minnows and night crawlers _ _ _ _ _ _ _ _ _
7. Prevents fish from chewing through the line _ _ _ _ _ _ _
8. Synonymous with fishing _ _ _ _ _ _ _ _
9. Red and white floating objects **B O B B E R**
10. Brings the fish in from water _ _ _ _ _ _ _ _ _ _ _
11. To be on a boat _ _ _ _ _ _ _
12. Boneless fish _ _ _ _ _ _ _
13. Describes several types of bass _ _ _ _ _ _ _ _ _ _
14. Hooks and weights fastened together _ _ _ _ _ _ _ _ _ _
15. A great or treasured spot _ _ _ _ _ _ _ _ _ _
16. Commercial fishing boat in the movie *The Perfect Storm* _ _ _ _ _ _ _ _
17. Most popular type of fishing in the US _ _ _ _ _ _ _ _ _ _ _
Scramble: Knot used to tie monofilament to braid _ _ _ _ _ _ _ _ _

Difficulty: ★★★☆☆

C	I	N	R	Z	L	R	E	L	L	■	L	A	O	R
P	M	U	O	J	B	C	B	O	C	V	L	V	T	S
E	E	P	O	F	D	B	V	I	Y	K	M	I	C	V
M	I	I	I	A	I	L	O	E	P	Y	B	M	Z	
R	M	M	S	V	U	Y	O	S	Y	U	I	V	T	M
D	H	M	B	I	J	V	D	A	W	R	I	L	V	U
G	U	A	Z	N	N	F	K	H	■	J	N	A	■	E
A	H	X	M	Q	E	O	R	Y	T	A	R	X	E	X
I	S	E	O	A	A	Z	■	A	N	■	G	I	T	T
F	O	L	A	G	D	D	T	G	O	T	A	V	E	■
X	H	D	O	S	M	O	N	V	G	G	V	A	D	N
D	R	A	M	K	J	M	B	M	Z	E	J	C	G	J
N	O	O	S	V	A	B	A	O	K	F	V	G	W	I
A	A	C	F	Q	D	W	U	O	V	Q	M	I	E	Q
T	I	E	F	K	E	N	C	H	I	K	T	W	D	A

G7100028

1. Mikasa, Molten, Wilson and Tachikara _ _ _ _ _ _ _ _ _ _ _ _
2. Inactive, passive _ _ _ _ _ _ _ _ _ _ _
3. A ruler, tyrant _ _ _ _ _ _ _ _ _
4. Hiroshima's car company _ _ _ _ _
5. The English-speaking world's oldest university _ _ _ _ _ _
6. An occupation, profession _ _ _ _ _ _ _ _ _ _
7. A Devilfish _ _ _ _ _ _ _ _
8. A foreigner or guest **V I S I T O R**
9. A command or decree _ _ _ _ _ _ _ _ _
10. Barcarolle's composer _ _ _ _ _ _ _ _ _ _
11. Boys, fathers, and men _ _ _ _ _ _
12. Professional baseball _ _ _ _ _ _ _ _ _ _ _ _ _
13. Host of the 2007 US Open _ _ _ _ _ _ _ _
14. Oil and vinegar dressing _ _ _ _ _ _ _ _ _ _ _ _
15. Prefecture covering hundreds of Japan's islands _ _ _ _ _ _ _ _
Scramble: South Africa and Madagascar's neighbor _ _ _ _ _ _ _ _ _ _

O	L	U	M	W	S	■	T	T	D	G	I	E	J	T
M	L	L	Ⓢ	K	A	A	C	P	Ⓐ	M	V	C	P	S
P	B	Y	V	H	Ⓐ	G	X	I	■	I	O	R	S	■
■	O	I	R	I	Y	K	A	■	Ⓐ	Q	Q	I	A	R
S	Z	E	■	S	L	V	A	E	R	I	W	C	S	Y
R	Z	I	Ⓢ	H	O	■	R	B	F	F	U	H	K	A
D	R	A	N	B	A	S	C	Ⓐ	A	L	A	U	D	S
D	C	L	K	T	U	J	R	J	C	N	■	T	G	A
Ⓐ	C	X	O	R	V	T	U	H	Z	Y	T	M	A	R
N	Z	I	Ⓢ	X̶	F̶	Ⓟ	P	I	A	■	C	Ⓢ	Ⓢ	S
Ⓒ	U	L	W	R	P	G	C	N	C	R	Ⓐ	Ⓒ	D	A
E	P	N	L	O	X	E	B	C	Ⓒ	K	Q	T	C	N
D	U	E	Ⓝ	Q̶	F̶	K̶	G̶	Ⓤ	O	L	G	E	B	■
F	J	T	Ⓣ	O̶	W̶	Ⓞ	R	S	Ⓢ	Ⓢ	Q	■	R	B	E
K	K	■	Ⓢ	O	I	■	I	F	Q	C	R	L	E	

G7000004

1. The ram of the stars _ _ _ _ _
2. The Man of Steel's inner reporter _ _ _ _ _ _ _ _ _
3. Heavenly spheres _ _ _ _ _ _
4. Violent explosion in a star's atmosphere _ _ _ _ _ _ _ _ _ _ _
5. A ringed celestial giant _ _ _ _ _ _ _
6. The archer of the heavens _ _ _ _ _ _ _ _ _ _ _
7. A constellation with a sting _ _ _ _ _ _ _ _
8. NASA's lunar program of the 60's _ _ _ _ _ _
9. The water-bearer of the zodiac _ _ _ _ _ _ _ _ _
10. Space travelers _ _ _ _ _ _ _ _ _ _
11. The crabby constellation _ _ _ _ _ _ _
12. Meteor's larger brother _ _ _ _ _ _ _ _
13. The Zodiac goat _ _ _ _ _ _ _ _ _ _
14. Time's Person of the 20th Century _ _ _ _ _ _ _
15. Dark points on stars **S U N S P O T S**
Scramble: Mankind's eyes over Saturn _ _ _ _ _ _ _

Difficulty: ★★★★☆

F	O	T	C	O	A		L	E	N	N	I	G	T	E
H	R	U	Ⓜ	J	J	A	P	B	Ⓗ	Y	V	F	E	I
X	K	G	G	X	Ⓞ	R	I	D	B	A	V	O	R	Z
E	D	A	L	S	Q	K	P	Ⓜ	F	A	A	V	H	
R	S		F	E	S	B	T	W	E		P	M		I
I	N	A	Ⓞ	O	Y	O	E	O	L	R	R	J	M	S
E	J	G	O	C	U	P	X	Ⓞ	T	S		L	M	L
Ⓦ	L	Ⓚ	B	C	R	M		E	U	F	E	H	E	Ⓗ
Ⓐ	E	Y	S	N	K	E		S	I	R	X	Q	L	O
	F	Ⓐ		N	P	G	R	O	K	N	A	T	R	
M	A	Ⓖ	U	D	S	Z	X	G	H	W	Ⓜ	Ⓗ	X	O
H	Ⓜ	Ⓜ	A	D	F	Y	Y	E	E	H	H	G	V	O
Z	Z	F	Ⓗ	A	I	F	I	C	S	Ⓞ	A	W	M	L
Q	I	C	O	Z	B	H	E	D	Z	P	C	N	Y	A
O	K	R	U		G	N	A	I	M	Ⓗ	R	Q	E	H

G7100010

1. A German theatre _ _ _ _ _ _ _ _ _
2. City on the West Lake of Chinese Zhejiang province _ _ _ _ _ _ _ _ _
3. Previous name for Yaren, capital of Nauru **M A K W A**
4. Pearl-producing-mollusk chowder _ _ _ _ _ _ _ _ _ _
5. Linux, Firefox, and Apache for example _ _ _ _ _ _ _ _ _ _
6. Bosnia's partner _ _ _ _ _ _ _ _ _ _ _
7. An equestrian "hair" behind the fetlock _ _ _ _ _ _ _ _ _ _ _ _ _
8. A hand wave or the "finger" _ _ _ _ _ _ _ _ _
9. Seaside beach resort in Argentina _ _ _ _ _ _ _ _ _ _ _ _
10. The oldest university in the English-speaking world _ _ _ _ _ _ _
11. The Thundering Herd _ _ _ _ _ _ _ _
12. 31st US President _ _ _ _ _ _ _
13. Popular destination city in East Java, Indonesia _ _ _ _ _ _ _
14. Overly controlling bosses _ _ _ _ _ _ _ _ _ _ _ _ _
Scramble: Barcarolle _ _ _ _ _ _ _ _ _ _

N	H	Y	H	D	A	N	A	A	B	L	P	O	T	A
Z	H	O	B	I	C	F	R	T	E	P	X	F	I	L
A	V	J	B	M	C	J	H	E	L	Z	B	O	F	R
L	V	U	L	E	O	F	A	Y	A	Q	V	O	N	Y
T	S	L	P		A	G	M	W	M	S	R	J	A	
D	E	E	Q	E	U	I	W	Y	W	L	P	O	K	U
	R	S	S	N	G	S	B	Q	L	M	C	G	C	G
T	P	I	A	V	J	C	B	K	S	A	E	T	R	C
C	U	X	W	I	G	U	Z	D	R	G	O	C	I	
S	A	Y	K	C	M	T	O	H	Z	I	M	Y	A	L
F	R	L	Q	K	L	I	E	U	H	G	T	I	F	A
L	Z	E	L	C	A	R	S	T	T	A	X	B	M	I
M	B	K	R	M	I	A	K	L	C	R	O	L	G	L
A	A	J	M	E	Q	G	R	J	A		V	A	C	K
N	U	M	W	Y	U	A	T	I	S	T	H	E	X	I

BB000001

1. Holds the brain _ _ _ _ _ _ _ _
2. Upper jaw _ _ _ _ _ _ _ _
3. Between the head and abdomen _ _ _ _ _ _ _
4. Where food is digested _ _ _ _ _ _ _ _
5. Small wrist bone _ _ _ _ _ _ _
6. System which provides the structure _ _ _ _ _ _ _ _ _
7. The brain's messenger _ _ _ _ _ _ _ _ _ _
8. Between the hip and knee _ _ _ _ _ _
9. Lower jaw, holds teeth in place _ _ _ _ _ _ _ _ _ _
10. Upper breastbone _ _ _ _ _ _ _ _ _
11. Used to lift objects above head _ _ _ _ _ _ _ _ _
12. The shinbone _ _ _ _ _ _
13. System which transports materials _ _ _ _ _ _ _ _ _ _ _
14. The smallest blood vessels _ _ _ _ _ _ _ _ _ _ _
15. The collar bone **C L A V I C L E**
16. Three types are hyaline, elastic, and fibrous _ _ _ _ _ _ _ _ _
17. Oval organ, major part of immune system _ _ _ _ _ _ _
Scramble: Broken by football players wearing cleats _ _ _ _ _ _ _ _ _ _ _

Difficulty: ★★★★☆

G7100032

1. Alpaca _ _ _ _ _ _
2. Aye or Nay _ _ _ _ _ _ _ _
3. To revere _ _ _ _ _ _ _ _ _
4. To cover, stuff _ _ _ _ _ _ _ _ _ _
5. Popular source of acidophilus _ _ _ _ _ _ _
6. Home to Tashkent _ _ _ _ _ _ _ _ _ _ _
7. The furthest boundary _ _ _ _ _ _
8. Desired, craved _ _ _ _ _ _ _ _
9. Large Mexican city on the Gulf of Mexico _ _ _ _ _ _ _ _ _
10. The best, matchless _ _ _ _ _ _ _ _ _ _ _ _ _
11. The Strip **L A S V E G A S**
12. The largest portion _ _ _ _ _ _ _ _ _ _ _
13. A wasp _ _ _ _ _ _ _ _ _ _ _ _ _
14. To snap or get angry _ _ _ _ _ _ _ _ _
15. Principles _ _ _ _ _ _ _
16. Thin spaghetti _ _ _ _ _ _ _ _ _ _
Scramble: Rain shields _ _ _ _ _ _ _ _ _ _

E	A	D	B	J	E	M	X	L	■	K	Y	A	W	V
Z	I	E	I	N	S	C	V	P	J	J	I	D	O	D
N	W	I	J	Z	I	P	G	U	■	E	D	N	S	T
■	S	M	■	R	O	A	E	E	O	F	J	W	M	■
R	E	■	A	M	B	B	R	K	C	■	R	J	Q	O
K	Q	O	J	O	C	E	K	T	M	R	G	P	T	L
P	I	P	V	Z	G	V	O	Y	O	W	C	X	I	N
P	U	S	R	A	C	A	■	F	Y	I	C	I	O	O
I	H	U	S	H	T	M	N	I	B	S	Z	D	T	S
X	Y	J	R	P	S	A	G	J	Y	A	A	T	N	■
V	A	I	H	H	Y	N	U	O	P	X	O	B	T	A
U	S	F	C	B	S	L	Q	F	L	R	A	Z	U	K
K	C	H	J	A	R	L	J	J	A	O	J	E	R	A
L	O	L	S	F	R	E	I	O	Q	L	E	W	S	K
O	R	D	E	■	D	Y	T	E	J	J	I	L	I	C

G7000007

1. The Father of Science Fiction _ _ _ _ _ _ _ _ _ _ _
2. An ancient Egyptian monolith _ _ _ _ _ _ _ _
3. BVI home of Foxy's and the Soggy Dollar _ _ _ _ _ _ _ _ _ _ _
4. Site of the Daily Double J E O P A R D Y
5. The Greek O _ _ _ _ _ _ _ _
6. The principle "law of succinctness" _ _ _ _ _ _ _ _ _ _ _ _
7. Carroll's nonsense poem _ _ _ _ _ _ _ _ _ _ _
8. Oriental flower for tea, perfumes, incense, and gardens _ _ _ _ _ _ _
9. A system of ruling by a few _ _ _ _ _ _ _ _ _ _
10. NYC's famous performing arts conservatory _ _ _ _ _ _ _ _ _
11. Capital of Indonesia _ _ _ _ _ _ _ _
12. The military's helicopter plane _ _ _ _ _ _ _
13. The process of bone formation _ _ _ _ _ _ _ _ _ _ _ _
14. A culture of sushi and sake _ _ _ _ _ _ _ _
Scramble: The eye's blind spot _ _ _ _ _ _ _ _ _

Difficulty: ★★★★★

M	E	J	A	W	C	M		A	C	E	U	O	P	H
C	T	Z	J	Y	B	C	A	K	L	V	X	O	W	C
O	U	I	K	U	J	J	F	D	N	P	O	T	T	
A	Q	O	P	G	J	O	N	Y	Z	W	E	O	C	I
U	G	O	L	B		L		V	N	H	H	I	A	Y
S	K	N	B	I	O	N	A	L	A	E	D	W	Q	X
X	O	Z	D	S	E	N	S	G	U	M	M	A	L	I
L	L	K	V	L	A		U	C	H	U	K	E	L	
R	L	F	I	T	S	K	Y	N	V	A	I	A	P	S
	V	O	T	I	P	R	B	F	U	I	L	K	R	N
A	D	I	E	M	U	T	R	M	Q		B	E	O	Z
U	Z	H	H	F	N	A	A	M	M	H	H	B	I	H
X	E	M	R	V	E	L	L	T	L	F	N	O	K	R
L	S	J	D	A	H	X	B	T	E	E	G	F		B
A	G	N	U		O	L	N	O	S	L	L	I	E	C

G7100008

1. Landlocked country surrounded by South Africa _ _ _ _ _ _ _ _
2. A fisherman _ _ _ _ _ _ _
3. The northernmost city in Latin America _ _ _ _ _ _ _ _ _
4. Niger's capital _ _ _ _ _ _ _
5. Large copper-mining city in the Congo _ _ _ _ _ _ _ _ _ _ _ _
6. Kenya's "Green City in the Sun" _ _ _ _ _ _ _ _
7. City on the shores of Lake Geneva _ _ _ _ _ _ _ _ _ _
8. Capital of Mayotte near Madagascar M A M O U T Z O U
9. Siberia's largest city _ _ _ _ _ _ _ _ _ _ _ _ _
10. Capital of Lesotho _ _ _ _ _ _ _
11. Flowers Delphinium and Consolida _ _ _ _ _ _ _ _ _
12. Slovenia's capital _ _ _ _ _ _ _ _ _ _
13. Spiritual energy _ _ _ _ _ _ _ _ _
14. Southernmost of the three Baltic states _ _ _ _ _ _ _ _ _ _
15. Mauritania's largest city _ _ _ _ _ _ _ _ _ _ _
Scramble: Romania and Ukraine's neighbor _ _ _ _ _ _ _

T	D	R	A	D	A	S	E	K	I	U	L	T	O	N
E	L	J	N	H	H	P	Y	M	V	Z	V	Y	L	A
U	M	O	H	V	Q	H	S	O	S	G	R	R	I	Y
I	M	D	C	M	G	F	A	T	M	G	K	F	W	J
M	K	■	X	E	W	S	P	■	G	U	V	B	H	N
C	Z	I	C	G	G	C	A	E	Q	R	Y	E	T	A
U	R	R	K	■	C	O	R	K	P	R	■	C	E	D
K	B	Y	■	O	E	L	G	S	I	G	O	F	Q	R
S	U	G	W	D	V	X	D	P	O	K	U	O	S	E
E	O	R	D	D	O	E	D	P	H	D	L	L	D	A
M	M	O	S	T	S	A	A	N	D	O	M	X	W	T
H	T	■	D	D	T	R	E	G	■	D	X	I	J	C
R	D	O	B	D	A	E	S	S	G	E	P	A	J	B
N	F	I	P	Y	W	I	C	R	N	J	V	E	Z	Y
C	P	E	E	A	R	■	L	Q	I	D	N	U	N	U

G7000008

1. Evolution's father _ _ _ _ _ _
2. A bishop's territory _ _ _ _ _ _ _ _
3. Bad liquor **R O T G U T**
4. Fifteen line French poetry _ _ _ _ _ _ _ _
5. Nixon's unknown nemesis _ _ _ _ _ _ _ _ _ _ _
6. A Celtic priest _ _ _ _ _ _
7. The capital of Iceland _ _ _ _ _ _ _ _ _
8. A notice of departure _ _ _ _ _ _ _ _ _ _ _
9. Your look-alike or double _ _ _ _ _ _ _ _ _ _ _ _ _
10. Not a QWERTY fan _ _ _ _ _ _ _
11. A deflection or rebound _ _ _ _ _ _ _ _
12. A sweet variety from the Rhine _ _ _ _ _ _ _ _ _
13. Moses' adopted brother _ _ _ _ _ _ _ _ _
14. Brought us *Crime and Punishment* _ _ _ _ _ _ _ _ _ _ _
15. A Montague _ _ _ _ _ _
16. A round building _ _ _ _ _ _ _ _
Scramble: The capital of Syria _ _ _ _ _ _ _ _ _

Difficulty: ★★★★★

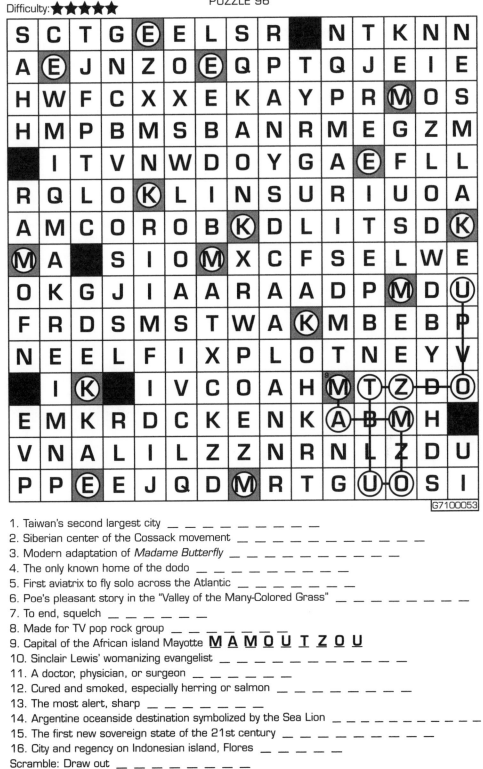

1. Taiwan's second largest city _ _ _ _ _ _ _ _ _
2. Siberian center of the Cossack movement _ _ _ _ _ _ _ _ _ _ _ _
3. Modern adaptation of *Madame Butterfly* _ _ _ _ _ _ _ _ _ _ _
4. The only known home of the dodo _ _ _ _ _ _ _ _ _ _
5. First aviatrix to fly solo across the Atlantic _ _ _ _ _ _ _ _
6. Poe's pleasant story in the "Valley of the Many-Colored Grass" _ _ _ _ _ _ _ _ _
7. To end, squelch _ _ _ _ _ _ _
8. Made for TV pop rock group _ _ _ _ _ _ _ _
9. Capital of the African island Mayotte M A M O U T Z O U
10. Sinclair Lewis' womanizing evangelist _ _ _ _ _ _ _ _ _ _ _
11. A doctor, physician, or surgeon _ _ _ _ _ _ _
12. Cured and smoked, especially herring or salmon _ _ _ _ _ _ _ _
13. The most alert, sharp _ _ _ _ _ _ _
14. Argentine oceanside destination symbolized by the Sea Lion _ _ _ _ _ _ _ _ _ _ _ _ _
15. The first new sovereign state of the 21st century _ _ _ _ _ _ _ _ _ _
16. City and regency on Indonesian island, Flores _ _ _ _ _ _
Scramble: Draw out _ _ _ _ _ _ _ _

SOLUTION TO PUZZLE 1: Outdoor Activities

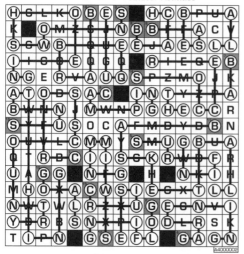

1. CROSSCOUNTRY	7. BATHE	13. SUNBATHING
2. GOLFING	8. CAMPING	14. SOCCER
3. SNOWSHOEING	9. BEACH	15. CRUISE
4. GARDENING	10. GOALS	16. BARBEQUE
5. SURFING	11. BASKETBALL	Scramble: CONCERTS
6. BASEBALL	12. SWIMMING	

SOLUTION TO PUZZLE 2

1. NOISE	7. LAUGHTER	13. NURSE
2. LOBSTERS	8. COWBOYHAT	14. LIZARD
3. COCONUT	9. NECKLACE	15. NORTHDAKOTA
4. HUNCHBACK	10. CYCLONE	16. CORNONTHECOB
5. SPIDERMAN	11. SANTACLAUS	Scramble: HOSPITAL
6. SEALEVEL	12. HUMMINGBIRD	

SOLUTION TO PUZZLE 3: Basketball

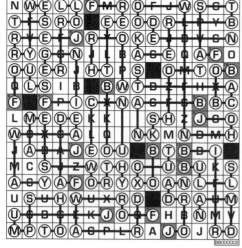

1. BOUNCE	7. BOXOUT	13. JAMESWORTHY
2. JOHNWOODEN	8. JUMPSHOT	14. BULLS
3. FASTBREAK	9. FINGERROLL	15. FORWARD
4. JERRYWEST	10. JORDAN	16. BOBCATS
5. BANKSHOT	11. FADEAWAY	17. BIRDMAN
6. FOULS	12. FREETHROW	Scramble: JIMCALHOUN

SOLUTION TO PUZZLE 4

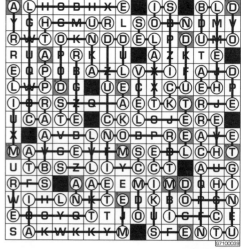

1. MEATBALLS	7. DONUT	13. ARTHUR
2. TELEVISION	8. APPLE	14. MIRACLE
3. ESKIMO	9. EMAIL	15. ELECTRONICS
4. DONALDDUCK	10. TEACHER	16. DUCKTALES
5. ANTEATERS	11. DOUBLEHEADER	Scramble: TURTLES
6. MICHIGAN	12. EASTER	

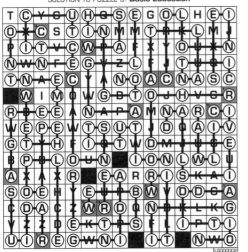

1. COLONIES
2. WETHEPEOPLE
3. ADDITION
4. RHODEISLAND
5. WRITING
6. CONSTITUTION
7. AGREEMENT
8. WASHINGTON
9. RADIUS
10. READING
11. ATLANTIC
12. ANGLE
13. CONNECTICUT
14. CIVILWAR
15. WEBSTER
Scramble: RIGHTS

1. GLOBE
2. FEATHER
3. BUTTERSCOTCH
4. GOLFCLUBS
5. OSTRICHES
6. PUMPKIN
7. BANANA
8. FUNNYBONE
9. PAJAMAS
10. GRAPEFRUIT
11. BUBBLEBATH
12. OXYGEN
13. POPCORNPOPPER
14. FUDGE
15. BULLSEYE
16. GENERALS
17. OVENS
Scramble: FITNESS

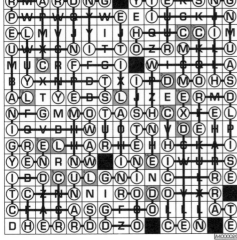

1. CHORES
2. DISHWASHING
3. ENERGY
4. LUNCH
5. CREDITCARDS
6. LAWNMOWING
7. DOGDOOR
8. DECORATE
9. CARPETING
10. COMMUNITY
11. LIFESTYLE
12. LAUNDRY
13. CHILDREN
14. ENTERTAINING
15. EXERCISE
Scramble: DINNERTIME

1. REDRIDING
2. WORLDCUP
3. INVENTION
4. KINGDOM
5. RULER
6. IGLOOS
7. KILLERWHALE
8. WEIGHT
9. WILDLIFE
10. ICECREAM
11. KANGAROOS
12. RUBBERBAND
13. IDEAS
14. KIDNEYBEAN
15. KENTUCKY
16. WATERCOOLER
17. KISSED
Scramble: RASPBERRY

SOLUTION TO PUZZLE 9: **What's in your House**

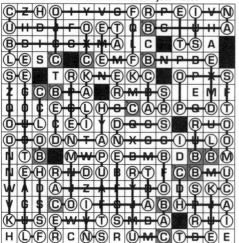

1. COUCH	7. BLINDS	13. BOOKSHELF
2. BUCKET	8. CLOSET	14. CURTAINS
3. BAKERSRACK	9. BEDPOST	15. CHAIRS
4. COMPUTER	10. COFFEETABLE	Scramble: CEDARCHEST
5. CHANDELIER	11. BASEBOARD	
6. BANISTER	12. BROOM	

SOLUTION TO PUZZLE 10

1. VOLCANO	7. WHEAT	13. HYDRANT
2. VENUS	8. VACATION	14. POLARBEAR
3. WISCONSIN	9. BUTTERFLIES	15. BABYSHOWERS
4. PEACOCK	10. WASHINGTON	16. HURRICANE
5. PORTUGAL	11. HUMMINGBIRD	Scramble: PENNSYLVANIA
6. BAMBOO	12. WATCHES	

SOLUTION TO PUZZLE 11: **Coffee Break**

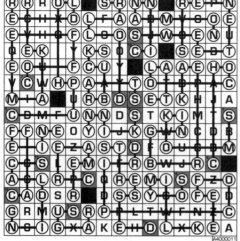

1. STARBUCKS	7. COFFEEMAKER	13. DRIPCOFFEE
2. SMOKINGBREAK	8. SWEETENERS	14. DESSERTS
3. SUGAR	9. SKINNY	15. SCALDING
4. SOYMILK	10. CREAMER	16. CINNAMON
5. CUPHOLDER	11. DOLLARS	Scramble: DARKROAST
6. CHOCOLATE	12. CAFFEINE	

SOLUTION TO PUZZLE 12: **Office Space**

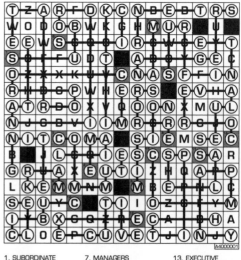

1. SUBORDINATE	7. MANAGERS	13. EXECUTIVE
2. EMAIL	8. SICKTIME	14. COREVALUES
3. CORPORATE	9. MISSION	15. COMPANY
4. ERRORS	10. SURFINTERNET	Scramble: MAILROOM
5. COMMUTE	11. SALESPITCH	
6. MARKETING	12. CUBICLES	

SOLUTION TO PUZZLE 13

1. RAINFALL
2. PEARL
3. JACKANDJILL
4. RELATIONSHIP
5. JEALOUSY
6. PUPPET
7. PRIMETIME
8. JOEYS
9. RABBITEARS
10. JELLYBEAN
11. PLATINUM
12. PRETZEL
13. POINSETTIA
14. RAGDOLL
15. ROCKINGCHAIR
Scramble: JUNCTION

SOLUTION TO PUZZLE 14: **Down on the Farm**

1. THISTLES
2. CATTLE
3. PRODUCTIVE
4. COWHERD
5. CALVINGTIME
6. TUMBLEWEED
7. TRACTOR
8. PASTURE
9. CAPACITY
10. PLANNING
11. TRADITIONS
12. CHORES
13. PAINT
14. PICKUPTRUCK
Scramble: TRITICALE

SOLUTION TO PUZZLE 15

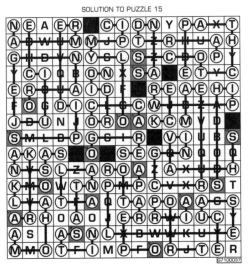

1. ATLANTA
2. AIRPORT
3. OLYMPIC
4. SCOTCHTAPE
5. OPERATOR
6. SANDTRAP
7. APPLESAUCE
8. SATIN
9. ACCORDION
10. SHAVINGCREAM
11. ARKANSAS
12. OKLAHOMA
13. SPIDERMAN
14. SHIPWRECK
15. ORANGEJUICE
16. OGRES
Scramble: ASTRONOMY

SOLUTION TO PUZZLE 16: **World Traveler**

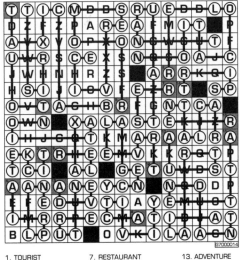

1. TOURIST
2. RELOCATION
3. TICKET
4. AIRPLANE
5. ROOMSERVICE
6. ACTIVITY
7. RESTAURANT
8. TAXICAB
9. RELAXATION
10. AUSTRALIA
11. ATTENDANT
12. TRAVELAGENCY
13. ADVENTURE
14. TRIPS
15. RENTALCAR
Scramble: ABROAD

SOLUTION TO PUZZLE 17

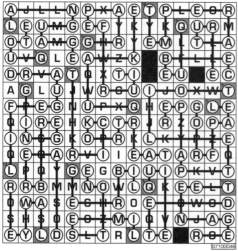

1. QUAKE	7. LAWYER	13. LIFEGUARD
2. LEAPFROG	8. QUOTE	14. QUEBEC
3. GERBIL	9. QUIETED	15. LIMESTONE
4. TRICKORTREAT	10. LANGUAGE	16. TEMPERATURE
5. GRAPEFRUIT	11. TEENAGER	Scramble: GORILLA
6. TOILETPAPER	12. GINGERBREAD	

SOLUTION TO PUZZLE 18: Music

1. AWARD	7. INSTRUMENT	13. AMERICANIDOL
2. ITUNES	8. RETAILER	14. SONYMUSIC
3. REMASTER	9. IMITATIONS	15. INTERNET
4. STRINGQUARTET	10. STARBUCKS	Scramble: ROCKANDROLL
5. SHUFFLE	11. ACOUSTIC	
6. AMATEUR	12. ROLLINGSTONES	

SOLUTION TO PUZZLE 19

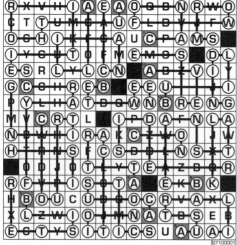

1. CANOFWORMS	7. COURTING	13. CONSIDER
2. BETWEEN	8. ATTRACTION	14. ALLIANCE
3. AUTHORITIES	9. BEANSTALK	Scramble: CULTURE
4. ACOUSTICS	10. BUILDING	
5. BLISTER	11. AVERSE	
6. AUSTRALIA	12. CRAYFISH	

SOLUTION TO PUZZLE 20: Greatest Players

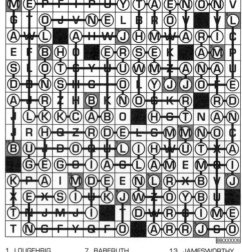

1. LOUGEHRIG	7. BABERUTH	13. JAMESWORTHY
2. BONDS	8. JOEMONTANA	14. MUHAMMEDALI
3. MARINO	9. JONES	15. BARKLEY
4. JOENAMATH	10. MIKEDITKA	16. MALONE
5. LARRYBIRD	11. JIMBROWN	Scramble: LEETREVINO
6. LEONARD	12. JACKSON	

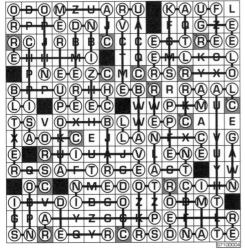

Puzzle 21

1. FLAMINGOS	7. ILLITERATE	13. IRELAND
2. INFIELDER	8. FAVOR	14. FREEZER
3. INFOMERCIAL	9. ARRESTS	15. ARNOLDPALMER
4. ALLSTARS	10. AFRAID	Scramble: ITINERARY
5. FOULBALL	11. FERRISWHEEL	
6. INTIMATE	12. ASSIST	

Puzzle 22

1. WINDSHIELD	7. SUNROOF	13. WHEELS
2. SAFETYBELT	8. CLUTCH	14. CDPLAYER
3. DOORS	9. COOLANT	15. DASHBOARD
4. WATERPUMP	10. SECURITY	16. STEERINGWHEEL
5. DIPSTICK	11. CUPHOLDER	Scramble: DRIVESHAFT
6. WIPERBLADES	12. CARBURETOR	

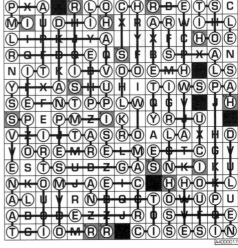

Puzzle 23

1. RIVERBOAT	7. CURVEBALL	13. CZECHREPUBLIC
2. RAPTORS	8. ROMANCING	14. REFUGEE
3. COINED	9. CLATTERED	15. CAMEROON
4. REINDEER	10. ROLLERSKATE	Scramble: REVEAL
5. CRAMP	11. COASTERS	
6. REPENTANCE	12. CONSIDER	

Puzzle 24

1. SPORTSGAMES	7. HOLIDAYS	13. IMPATIENT
2. INLAWS	8. RECREATIONAL	14. REHEARSALS
3. HOSTILE	9. RIVAL	15. SCHOOLWORK
4. IMPERATIVE	10. HAPPINESS	Scramble: INSURANCE
5. SUPPER	11. HOUSEHOLD	
6. ROMANTIC	12. SECURITY	

SOLUTION TO PUZZLE 25

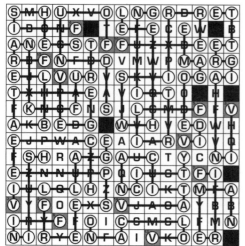

1. VIDEOGAME
2. FREESPEECH
3. VILLAGE
4. FISHES
5. FLIRTING
6. FINISH
7. FIREMAN
8. VINAIGRETTE
9. VEGETABLE
10. FERRISWHEEL
11. FOUNDS
12. VOLCANO
13. FRANKFURT
14. VATICANCITY
Scramble: VICTORIA

SOLUTION TO PUZZLE 26: **Romantic Dinner**

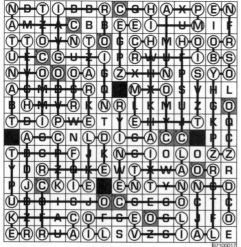

1. VEGETABLE
2. WASABI
3. KIWIFRUIT
4. WALNUTS
5. VINAIGRETTE
6. KABOBS
7. WATERMELON
8. VEALPARMESAN
9. WILDRICE
10. VENISON
11. KOBEBEEF
12. KALAMATA
13. KINGCRAB
14. WHEAT
15. KEYLIMEPIE
Scramble: VINEGAR

SOLUTION TO PUZZLE 27

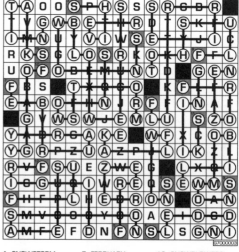

1. CHIMPANZEE
2. COMETS
3. OUTFIELDER
4. OLIVEOIL
5. OPERATION
6. CUTTHROAT
7. ORLANDO
8. CRACKERJACK
9. CHOIRCHAIR
10. ORIGIN
11. CANTON
12. CONTINENTAL
13. OZZYOSBORNE
Scramble: ORIONSBELT

SOLUTION TO PUZZLE 28: **Old Man Winter**

1. SNOWSTORM
2. SHIVER
3. SNOWMOBILE
4. SLEDDING
5. FREEZER
6. FLUSHOT
7. FEBRUARY
8. SNOWFLAKE
9. FLURRIES
10. FOGGY
11. SKIING
12. FRIGID
13. SNOWBLOWERS
14. FLUSEASON
15. SKATING
16. FROZEN
Scramble: FOURSEASONS

SOLUTION TO PUZZLE 29

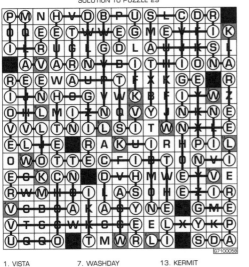

1. VISTA	7. WASHDAY	13. KERMIT
2. LILYPADS	8. KINDHEARTED	14. LINGERIE
3. KANSASCITY	9. LIGHTNINGBUG	15. WINNIPEG
4. VANCOUVER	10. KINETIC	16. VENEER
5. WOLVERINE	11. WEIRDO	Scramble: WATERMELON
6. LOVELETTER	12. VAMPIRE	

SOLUTION TO PUZZLE 30: **Fun in the Sun**

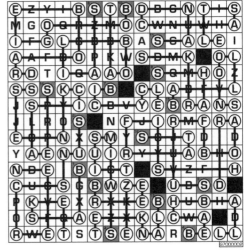

1. BASKET	7. BICYCLE	13. BLANKET
2. SWIMSUIT	8. SHARKS	14. SEASICKNESS
3. SUNSCREEN	9. SAILBOAT	15. BALLOONS
4. BEACHBALL	10. BOOGIEBOARD	Scramble: STINGRAY
5. BREEZE	11. SANDCASTLE	
6. SURFBOARD	12. STARFISH	

SOLUTION TO PUZZLE 31: **Cats**

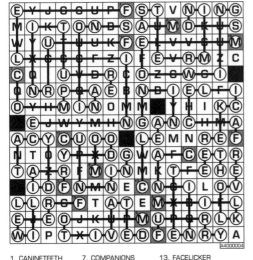

1. CANINETEETH	7. COMPANIONS	13. FACELICKER
2. MILKLOVER	8. MOTIVATED	14. FURNITURE
3. FRAIDYCAT	9. MASTERMINDS	15. MEOWING
4. FELINE	10. CLEANING	Scramble: CONTEMPLATIVE
5. MOODY	11. CUNNING	
6. FURRY	12. FREEWILL	

SOLUTION TO PUZZLE 32

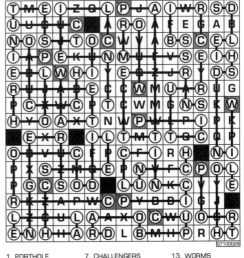

1. PORTHOLE	7. CHALLENGERS	13. WORMS
2. CROCODILES	8. WATERHOLE	14. WINDSHIELDS
3. CUTEST	9. CUPBOARD	Scramble: WRANGLER
4. PATTERNS	10. PICNICLUNCH	
5. CLIENT	11. PICTURE	
6. PINOCCHIO	12. CRIBS	

SOLUTION TO PUZZLE 33: At the Beach

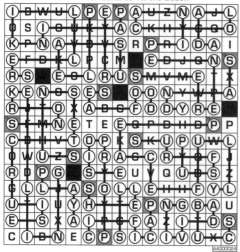

1. SURFSUP	7. SCUBADIVING
2. PORPOISE	8. PLAYA
3. SEAFOOD	9. SERENE
4. PLEASURE	10. SUNSETCRUISE
5. PACIFIC	11. PINACOLADA
6. SHELLS	12. SNORKELING

13. SANDY
14. PAINKILLERS
15. PEACEFULLY
Scramble: PICTURESQUE

SOLUTION TO PUZZLE 34

1. FRENCHHORN	7. STOVE
2. FLOPPED	8. FERRISWHEELS
3. SHELF	9. SUDDENLY
4. FOUROCLOCKS	10. FRANKFURT
5. FLESH	11. FAIRYTALE
6. SCORPION	12. SOUTHDAKOTA

13. SLOVAKIA
14. SWEETSPOTS
Scramble: FRAGILE

SOLUTION TO PUZZLE 35: Car Buying

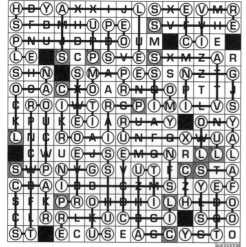

1. COMPROMISE	7. SAFETY
2. LICENSING	8. LUXURY
3. SALESPEOPLE	9. SPORTSCAR
4. SAVINGS	10. CHOOSY
5. PUSHY	11. SERVICES
6. LOYAL	12. LOANS

13. CAUTIOUS
14. PRESSURE
15. PRIORITIES
Scramble: CUSTOMERCARE

SOLUTION TO PUZZLE 36

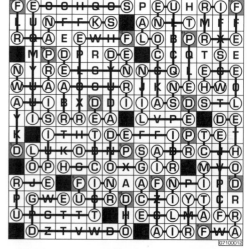

1. DEADENED	7. PRAIRIEDOGS
2. DOMINICA	8. DELINQUENT
3. FAIRYTALE	9. POLOPITCH
4. FARFETCHED	10. FERRARI
5. DAISIES	11. PENSACOLA
6. FURNITURE	12. FERRISWHEELS

13. FRANKS
14. PRAWN
15. DODGE
Scramble: PARTHREE

SOLUTION TO PUZZLE 37: Office Supplies

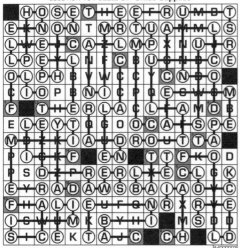

1. FOLIO
2. CHAIR
3. CALCULATOR
4. DONUTS
5. COMPUTER
6. CABINET
7. TAPEMEASURE
8. CELLPHONE
9. CLOCK
10. FACSIMILE
11. FOLDERS
12. TABLET
13. TELEPHONES
14. FILEDRAWERS
15. CALENDAR
16. DAYTIMER
17. TERMINAL
Scramble: DESKTOP

SOLUTION TO PUZZLE 38

1. AUGUSTA
2. UMPIRE
3. ALLERGIES
4. EXPANSION
5. ALBANY
6. UZBEKISTAN
7. UNITEDARAB
8. ANGRY
9. EVENINGS
10. UNCLESAM
11. AMPERAGE
12. CONSTRICTOR
13. EASTERISLAND
14. ELSALVADOR
15. COUNT
Scramble: CLUBHOUSE

SOLUTION TO PUZZLE 39: Vacation Destinations

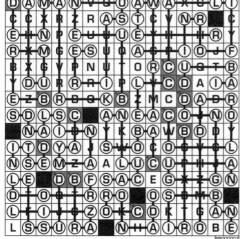

1. DUBAI
2. BUENOSAIRES
3. DESTIN
4. BRAZIL
5. CALIFORNIA
6. DENMARK
7. CAYMANISLANDS
8. CABOSANLUCAS
9. BERMUDA
10. COLORADO
11. BRISBANE
12. CLEARWATER
13. DUSSELDORF
14. CORONADO
15. DONGGUAN
Scramble: BARCELONA

SOLUTION TO PUZZLE 40

1. RENDER
2. GOLFBALL
3. RERUN
4. GUACAMOLE
5. GLIMMERED
6. RELIABILITY
7. GRENADE
8. GAINFUL
9. RESOLVE
10. RENTALCAR
11. RECHARGE
12. ROLLERCOASTER
13. GREATBRITAIN
14. GOTMILK
15. REDUCTION
Scramble: GOVERNOR

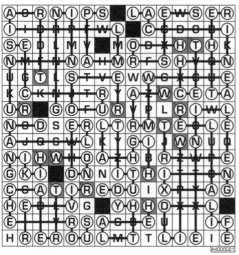

1. HEALTHY	7. WILDLIFE	13. RIVER
2. RESOURCES	8. WONDERLAND	14. HIKING
3. RUNNING	9. TRAILMAPS	15. TECHNICAL
4. TREACHEROUS	10. HIGHALTITUDE	Scramble: WHISTLING
5. WARMWEATHER	11. HORSES	
6. RELAXING	12. TREELINE	

1. FIRSTPITCHES	7. FEBRUARY	13. THOUSANDS
2. FOURSOMES	8. TROLLEYING	14. WHISTLE
3. THUNDER	9. WAIST	15. FRANCE
4. SIDEWALK	10. SKINKS	16. WHERE
5. TIJUANA	11. SONGS	Scramble: SANFRANCISCO
6. WOODPECKERS	12. FLUENTLY	

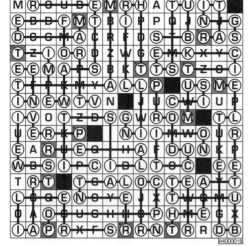

1. TRAILERS	7. RATINGS	13. TICKETSTUBS
2. MELTEDBUTTER	8. PREVIEWS	14. REALISTIC
3. PRODUCTION	9. POPCORN	15. TIMEWASTER
4. RENTAL	10. MADEFORTV	Scramble: PARAMOUNT
5. THEATER	11. MUSIC	
6. THRILLING	12. MATINEE	

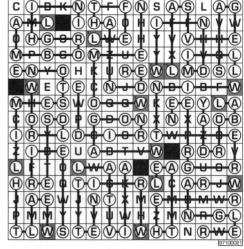

1. LIMESTONE	7. WRANGLER	13. LASVEGAS
2. WINDMILL	8. LEFTHANDER	14. LATVIA
3. WAGONRIDE	9. WOMEN	15. LABORDAY
4. LAMBORGHINI	10. LEATHER	Scramble: LUNCHES
5. WORLDSERIES	11. WINTERGREEN	
6. WRITTEN	12. WEALTH	

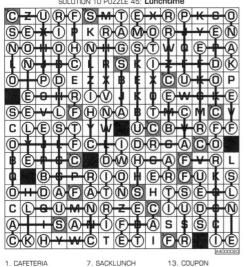

1. CAFETERIA	7. SACKLUNCH	13. COUPON
2. FRIENDS	8. CREDITCARD	14. CELEBRATION
3. FRUITS	9. FRENCHFRIES	15. STARVING
4. COFFEEBREAK	10. SANDWICH	16. CUPONOODLES
5. CUSTOMER	11. FUELS	Scramble: SPLITCHECK
6. FASTFOOD	12. SHARE	

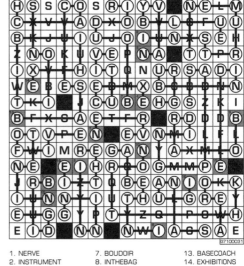

1. NERVE	7. BOUDOIR	13. BASECOACH
2. INSTRUMENT	8. INTHEBAG	14. EXHIBITIONS
3. NAVYBLUE	9. INNING	15. NINETOFIVE
4. EXECUTIVE	10. NORTHKOREA	16. EITHER
5. BRIDGE	11. EDINBURGH	Scramble: NEMESIS
6. BOARDINGPASS	12. IGUANAS	

1. CARPOOL	7. COMMUTING	13. CHANGINGLANES
2. REACTING	8. CRASHES	14. TIRED
3. CARTROUBLE	9. TOWTRUCK	15. STUCK
4. TAILLIGHTS	10. CUTOFF	16. SNOWPLOWING
5. SIGNAL	11. RUNNINGLATE	17. TRACTION
6. RUSHHOUR	12. RADIO	Scramble: STOPANDGO

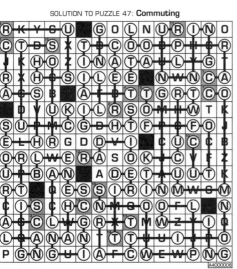

1. INTEGRAL	7. HOTSEAT	13. NICARAGUA
2. NOTRE	8. HORNETSNEST	14. PROBLEM
3. POPULATE	9. PASSENGER	15. HAMBURGER
4. ICELAND	10. HARMONIES	Scramble: INDUSTRIES
5. HYENAS	11. POWERHOUSE	
6. INSTRUMENT	12. NEWJERSEY	

SOLUTION TO PUZZLE 49: **Vacation**

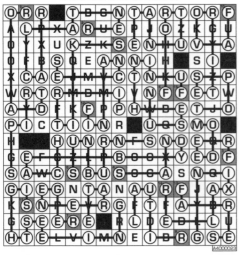

1. SKITRIP
2. RENTALCAR
3. FREEDOM
4. SANDYBEACH
5. ROADTRIPS
6. FORTUNATE
7. REGENERATE
8. SUNBURNS
9. RITUAL
10. FAVORITESPOT
11. SIGHTSEEING
12. FINANCES
13. FARES
14. RELAXING
15. FUNINTHESUN
Scramble: SUNSCREEN

SOLUTION TO PUZZLE 50

1. TRANSPORTING
2. QUIXOTE
3. XZIBIT
4. FOOTLOCKER
5. QUIVERS
6. XCHROMOSOME
7. TRADEMARK
8. TRUSTEE
9. QUOTIENT
10. XFILES
11. FIRSTKISS
12. QUADRATIC
13. THRONE
14. XANAX
15. FALLINGINLOVE
Scramble: FUNNELCAKES

SOLUTION TO PUZZLE 51: **Drinks**

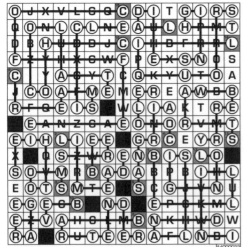

1. BELLINI
2. LIMEADE
3. SMOOTHIES
4. COOLER
5. BEERS
6. SANGRIA
7. LADIESNIGHT
8. BARTENDER
9. CREAMSICLE
10. BEVERAGE
11. STRAWBERRY
12. CHOCOLATE
13. LONGISLAND
14. LIQUORS
15. COFFEE
Scramble: SWEETTEA

SOLUTION TO PUZZLE 52

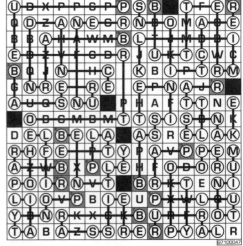

1. RURAL
2. BASSINET
3. BASERUNNER
4. RATTLESNAKE
5. PLUTONIUM
6. PLATE
7. BRASSIERE
8. BENTLEY
9. PONYTAIL
10. PUERTO
11. BARHOP
12. REACTIONS
13. BUTTERMILK
14. RIFLE
15. PARTYPOOPER
16. BARNDANCE
Scramble: RUBBERBAND

SOLUTION TO PUZZLE 53: **FORE!**

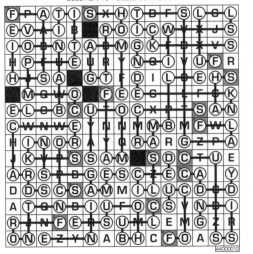

1. SHORTGAME	7. CLUBHOUSE	13. FASHIONABLE
2. FRONTNINE	8. COMPETITIVE	14. SLICED
3. CUSSING	9. FAMOUS	15. CADDY
4. SCRAMBLE	10. SKINSGAMES	16. SCORECARDS
5. FLAGSTICKS	11. SHANKED	Scramble: CAMARADERIE
6. FOCUS	12. FULLSWING	

SOLUTION TO PUZZLE 54

1. GRASSHOPPER	7. GLOVE	13. GERANIUMS
2. GREASE	8. NEUTRON	14. GIBRALTAR
3. GODPARENT	9. JESSEJAMES	15. NEANDERTHAL
4. GARFIELD	10. JERUSALEM	16. JOUST
5. NEWZEALAND	11. NATIONAL	Scramble: JESTER
6. NATURE	12. JERSEY	

SOLUTION TO PUZZLE 55: **DWTS**

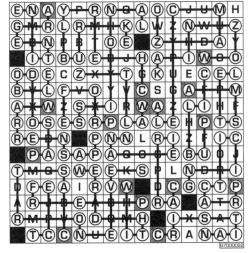

1. WARRENSAPP	7. CASTRONEVES	13. WOZNIAK
2. CARRIEANN	8. CRISTIAN	14. PRACTICING
3. ALECMAZO	9. PERFECT	15. CHERYLBURKE
4. PROFESSIONAL	10. ARGENTINE	16. PUBLIC
5. PASODOBLE	11. WITHDREW	Scramble: ACHILLES
6. WALTZ	12. AMSTEL	

SOLUTION TO PUZZLE 56

1. UNITS	7. QUOTIENT	13. UMBRELLA
2. KETCHUP	8. KLEENEX	14. UNCLESAM
3. QUIET	9. QUESTIONS	15. KOALAS
4. QUIVERS	10. KOMODODRAGON	16. KEYLIMEPIE
5. USUAL	11. KNOWLEDGE	Scramble: UPHEAVAL
6. KNOCKWURST	12. KETTLE	

SOLUTION TO PUZZLE 57: **Marriage**

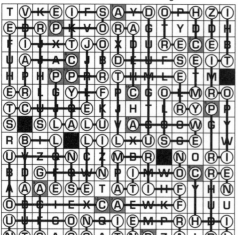

1. POSITIVE	7. ADULTERY	13. PLAYFUL
2. PARENTING	8. CAREERS	14. CARDS
3. AFFIRMATION	9. ACCOUNTABLE	Scramble: AUTHORITY
4. CHORE	10. PROJECTS	
5. PRIORITIZE	11. AWESOME	
6. CHILDREN	12. COUNSELING	

SOLUTION TO PUZZLE 58

1. ARITHMETIC	7. ARGENTINA	13. JOSEPH
2. ALLIGATOR	8. ENGAGED	14. EARTHQUAKES
3. JUGGERNAUT	9. JAMPACKED	15. EVERYSPRING
4. ESPECIALLY	10. ANGLE	Scramble: ARABIAN
5. ATHENS	11. ENVIRONMENT	
6. JAWBONES	12. JACKSONVILLE	

SOLUTION TO PUZZLE 59: **Harry and Hogwarts**

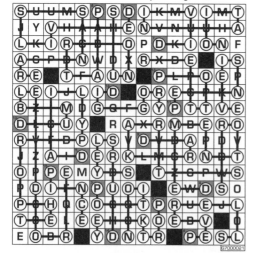

1. DEVILSSNARE	7. DIVINATION	13. POTTER
2. PORTKEY	8. PATRONUS	14. DURSLEYS
3. POTION	9. DARKARTS	15. PINCE
4. DEMENTORS	10. DUMBLEDORE	Scramble: POMFREY
5. DAILYPROPHET	11. PENSIEVE	
6. PEVERELLSEY	12. DIGGORY	

SOLUTION TO PUZZLE 60

1. WHALE	7. QUADRANT	13. SLOSH
2. WATERWINGS	8. SURFBOARD	14. QUARTER
3. QUESTIONS	9. WORLDRECORDS	15. SOUTHAFRICA
4. WOMEN	10. QUAYLE	16. QUEBEC
5. SORENSTAM	11. WORSTED	Scramble: SNOWBLOWER
6. STOMACH	12. WHITEGOLDOWER	

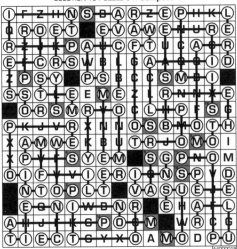

SOLUTION TO PUZZLE 61: **Computers**

1. MONITOR
2. POWERPOINT
3. PRINTERS
4. SPAMFILTER
5. SAVING
6. MOTHERBOARD
7. PROCESSOR
8. SAVESPACE
9. MOUSE
10. SOFTWARE
11. POPULAR
12. PATIENCE
13. SYSTEM
14. MEMORY
15. SPEED
16. SIMPLE
17. SERIALPORT
Scramble: MEDIA

SOLUTION TO PUZZLE 62: **Tea Time**

1. HOTPLATES
2. TEMPERATURE
3. CELESTIAL
4. TEAPOT
5. TAZOTEAS
6. HERBAL
7. HOTTOHANDLE
8. HOLISTIC
9. CHINA
10. SPOON
11. SLEEPYTIME
12. COFFEE
13. TEACUPS
14. SUGAR
15. HEALING
16. SIPPING
17. TOOTHSTAINING
Scramble: CHAMOMILE

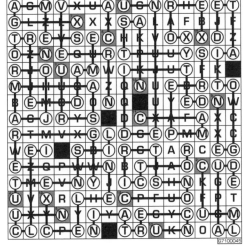

SOLUTION TO PUZZLE 63

1. UNEDITED
2. CUMLAUDE
3. UTENSIL
4. NOTREDAME
5. NUCLEI
6. CAVERN
7. XGAMES
8. NEGOTIATED
9. URSAMAJOR
10. UNCERTAIN
11. CAMPERS
12. XCELENERGY
13. CONSTRICTOR
14. NASTY
15. XEROX
Scramble: XFACTOR

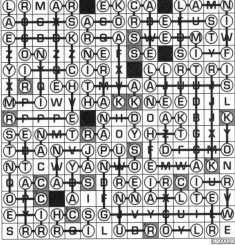

SOLUTION TO PUZZLE 64: **Idol**

1. REHEARSAL
2. CHRIS
3. SEACREST
4. RUNNERUP
5. KRISALLEN
6. RICKEYMINOR
7. KATHARINE
8. SEMIFINALS
9. KARAOKE
10. SONGWRITER
11. SANJAYA
12. CARRIE
13. RANDY
14. KODAKTHEATRE
15. CONTESTANT
16. CLAIROL
Scramble: SIMONCOWELL

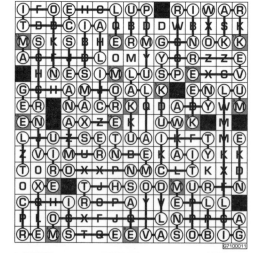

SOLUTION TO PUZZLE 65

1. HAPPENS
2. HIDEABED
3. INSURANCE
4. SPIDERMAN
5. THANK
6. SELECTION
7. THUMBELINA
8. HARRISON
9. SHRIMP
10. HOLLANDAISE
11. TEDDYBEARS
12. TALLAHASSEE
13. TEGUCIGALPA
14. IDAHO

Scramble: ILLINOIS

SOLUTION TO PUZZLE 66: **Wedding**

1. DREAMDAY
2. GROOM
3. DINNER
4. RAINORSHINE
5. GAFFE
6. PHOTOGRAPHY
7. DATING
8. REHEARSAL
9. RINGSHOPPING
10. PLANNER
11. REGISTRY
12. PRESENTS
13. DANCING
14. GLASSES
15. RELAXATION
16. PRINCESS

Scramble: GUESTLIST

SOLUTION TO PUZZLE 67

1. ELECTION
2. EXERCISE
3. KUWAITCITY
4. MOLDOVA
5. KUALALUMPUR
6. EARTHS
7. MICROMANAGERS
8. MELBOURNE
9. MULLIGANS
10. EVERYSPRING
11. KRAKOW
12. KENYA
13. MALAISES
14. EXAMRESULT
15. ENVIRONMENT

Scramble: KOMODO

SOLUTION TO PUZZLE 68: **BBQ**

1. GATHERING
2. SLIDERS
3. PORKCHOPS
4. PULLEDPORK
5. HANGOUT
6. GAMETIME
7. SALAD
8. PATIO
9. HOTTOHANDLE
10. GREASY
11. POTATOSALAD
12. HAMBURGER
13. GASGRILL
14. HAPPYHOUR
15. SWIMMINGPOOL

Scramble: SEASONINGS

SOLUTION TO PUZZLE 69

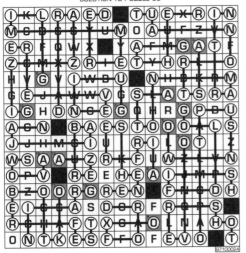

1. GATHER	7. GOLDFISH	13. GRAIN
2. GUINEVERE	8. GLIMMERED	14. AVOWS
3. ASTRONAUT	9. OXFORD	15. GIZZARD
4. OVERSHOT	10. AZERBAIJAN	Scramble: OFFSHORE
5. OWNSUPTO	11. OKTOBERFEST	
6. AIRFRESHENER	12. ASTONMARTIN	

SOLUTION TO PUZZLE 70: Let's Play

1. BOWANDARROW	7. FIGHTING	13. BATTINGCAGE
2. FLORIDA	8. FLYING	14. BATTERSBOX
3. BILLIARDS	9. FIELDHOCKEY	Scramble: FOOTBALL
4. FLOPSHOT	10. FRISBEE	
5. BASKETBALL	11. FISTS	
6. FREETHROW	12. BOARDING	

SOLUTION TO PUZZLE 71

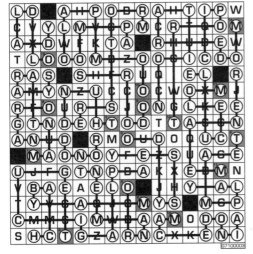

1. THUNDERSTORM	7. MANTARAYS	13. MOLECULE
2. MAYBACH	8. ODORS	14. MODERATION
3. ODYSSEY	9. ORGANDONOR	15. OLDLADY
4. TEGUCIGALPA	10. MACEDONIA	16. OOMPALOOMPA
5. ORNAMENT	11. MEANER	Scramble: TOMWATSON
6. TEAMPLAY	12. TROPIC	

SOLUTION TO PUZZLE 72: Investing 101

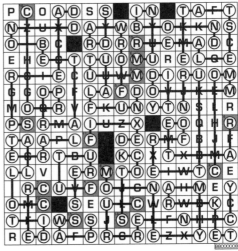

1. FUTURES	7. CREDIT	13. SWAPS
2. MUTUALFUND	8. MONEYMARKET	14. STOCK
3. COMMODITY	9. SPREAD	15. REALESTATE
4. RATEOFRETURN	10. CURRENCY	16. CORPORATEBOND
5. FORWARDS	11. FIXED	Scramble: REVERSEREPO
6. MUNIBOND	12. COLLATERAL	

SOLUTION TO PUZZLE 73

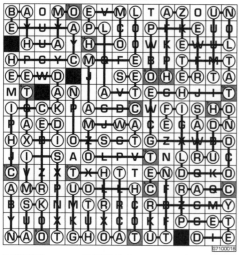

1. CARPETED
2. THROAT
3. CAMEL
4. CENTURY
5. HAZELNUT
6. TAXIDERMIST
7. HONDURAS
8. OKSANA
9. OPERETTA
10. THEGOODLIFE
11. THOUGHT
12. TOMWATSON
13. CHICKADEE
14. HOMEPLATES
15. OMAHABEACH
Scramble: OTTOMAN

SOLUTION TO PUZZLE 74: **Bicycling**

1. TANDEM
2. SPEED
3. GEOMETRY
4. GRANNYGEAR
5. STATIONARY
6. TIRES
7. GIRODITALIA
8. GROUPRIDE
9. GETAWAY
10. SCENERY
11. TEAMWORK
12. GASHES
13. SINGLETRACK
14. SPONSORSHIP
15. TRIATHLONS
16. SADDLE
Scramble: TECHNICAL

SOLUTION TO PUZZLE 75

1. JUNGLEBOOK
2. ZEPPELIN
3. OBSERVANT
4. JACKNICKLAUS
5. JAMESTOWN
6. ZIPPERS
7. JUNEBUGS
8. ADVENTUROUS
9. ARITHMETIC
10. ZAIRE
11. JEOPARDY
12. OASIS
13. ONCEUPONATIME
14. ORATOR
15. ACTIVITY
Scramble: ZEBRAFISHES

SOLUTION TO PUZZLE 76: **World War II**

1. GERMANY
2. GLOBAL
3. REFUGEES
4. HEDGEHOG
5. CHURCHILL
6. COMMUNISM
7. ADOLFHITLER
8. ARYAN
9. REICH
10. HIMMLER
11. HOMING
12. GRAFSPEE
13. GENEVA
14. AUSTRIA
15. RESISTANCE
16. CAPITALISM
17. GASCHAMBERS
Scramble: ASSAULTRIFLE

SOLUTION TO PUZZLE 77

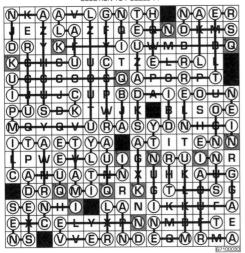

1. QUICKSAND
2. INTIMATE
3. KINGCRAB
4. QUARTER
5. NIAGARA
6. INCENSES
7. NETHERLANDS
8. KATYDIDS
9. QUAYLE
10. NINEONEONE
11. NEVERLAND
12. INSTRUMENT
13. QUADRATIC
14. KUALALUMPUR
Scramble: INTERPRETS

SOLUTION TO PUZZLE 78: **Health Check-Up**

1. COUNSELOR
2. EXERCISE
3. DIABETES
4. CALORIC
5. ENERGY
6. DETOXIFY
7. COUGHING
8. EPILEPTIC
9. DOCTOR
10. CHOLESTEROL
11. CARCINOGEN
12. EXAMS
13. DRUGSCREEN
14. DIETS
15. COLDS
Scramble: EMPHYSEMA

SOLUTION TO PUZZLE 79: **Health Foods**

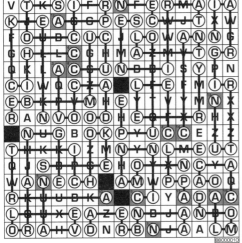

1. NAANBREAD
2. CELERY
3. AVOCADO
4. CHICKEN
5. NAVELORANGE
6. CUCUMBER
7. ALMOND
8. CINNAMON
9. NECTARINES
10. ARTICHOKES
11. APPLE
12. APRICOTS
13. NUTRIGRAIN
14. CANTALOUPE
15. CACAO
Scramble: NAVYBEAN

SOLUTION TO PUZZLE 80

1. WONDERED
2. WILLIAM
3. DEBEERS
4. DREDGING
5. GREGARIOUS
6. DECONSTRUCT
7. GRENADINE
8. DRONE
9. GIVEANDTAKE
10. WENCH
11. WINDEX
12. GLIMMERED
13. GARISH
14. DELPHI
15. WYATTEARP
Scramble: GERSHWIN

SOLUTION TO PUZZLE 81: Travel

1. LASTMINUTE
2. TOURISTTRAP
3. PLANNING
4. ADVENTURE
5. LUXURY
6. LODGING
7. TIRING
8. AIRLINES
9. LINES
10. ALLINCLUSIVE
11. TIMEZONE
12. PACKLIGHT
13. PHOTOGRAPHY
14. TAXICABS
15. PASSPORTS
16. TRAIN

Scramble: ANTICIPATION

SOLUTION TO PUZZLE 82

1. URCHIN
2. UPONTHEROOF
3. SCIMITAR
4. SPANGLISH
5. POSTPONE
6. STANLEY
7. PGTHIRTEEN
8. UPROOTED
9. UMATHURMAN
10. PAVLOV
11. SPRINGTIDE
12. SEATTLESLEW
13. PRONG
14. UNDERGO
15. PROHIBITION
16. UMBER

Scramble: PIMENTO

SOLUTION TO PUZZLE 83: DWTS

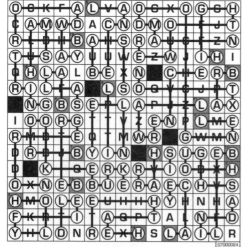

1. LACEY
2. HOUGHS
3. LENGOODMAN
4. BALLAS
5. HARRIS
6. LANCEBASS
7. BROOKEBURKE
8. HOLYFIELD
9. LINLEY
10. HIGHTOWER
11. LAWRENCE
12. BROADWAY
13. BERGERON
14. HEATHER
15. BRAXTON
16. HAMSTRING
17. BELINDA

Scramble: LISARINNA

SOLUTION TO PUZZLE 84

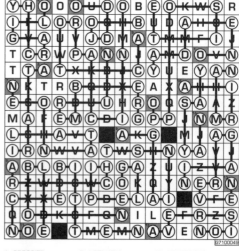

1. OPPOSITE
2. OLIGARCHY
3. ATARI
4. ONEADAY
5. ACTORPACINO
6. NUREMBERG
7. NEONATAL
8. ARCHIPELAGO
9. AGAINST
10. NOBLE
11. ONCEBITTEN
12. AVERSIONT
13. NEVERAGAIN
14. NAYSAY
15. ODDJOB
16. AIRMAN

Scramble: OTTMARLIEBERT

SOLUTION TO PUZZLE 85: **Michael Jackson**

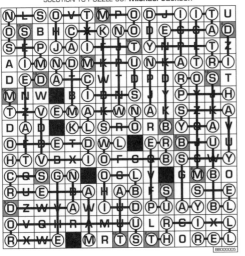

1. SUPERBOWL	7. SCREAM	13. TITOJACKSON
2. THRILLER	8. MORPH	14. MTVVIDEO
3. BUBBLES	9. DANGEROUS	15. TABLOID
4. DIRTYDIANA	10. MOONWALK	16. DEATH
5. MUSICANDME	11. SIMPSONS	Scramble: BADWORLDTOUR
6. BEATIT	12. SAYSAYSAY	

SOLUTION TO PUZZLE 86

1. UMBRELLA	7. WYOMING	13. TORREYPINES
2. UNCLESAM	8. WARSAW	14. WARRANTS
3. WHITEHORSE	9. USUAL	15. UPONTHEROOF
4. UPTURN	10. TAPESTRY	Scramble: WALLABY
5. TAJIKISTAN	11. TOSTADA	
6. TOGETHERS	12. WORLDSERIES	

SOLUTION TO PUZZLE 87: **Gone Fishing**

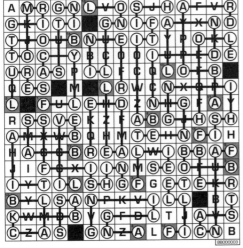

1. FLYCASTING	7. LEADER	13. BLACKBASS
2. LURES	8. ANGLING	14. BOTTOMRIG
3. FLIES	9. BOBBER	15. FISHINGHOLE
4. BAITFISH	10. LANDINGNET	16. LONGLINER
5. FANCAST	11. ABOARD	17. BASSFISHING
6. LIVEBAIT	12. FILLET	Scramble: ALBRIGHT

SOLUTION TO PUZZLE 88

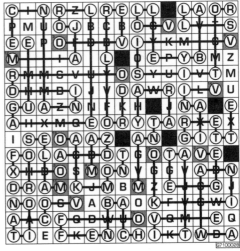

1. VOLLEYBALLS	7. MANTARAY	13. OAKMONT
2. VEGETATIVE	8. VISITOR	14. VINAIGRETTE
3. OVERLORD	9. ORDINANCE	15. OKINAWA
4. MAZDA	10. OFFENBACH	Scramble: MOZAMBIQUE
5. OXFORD	11. MALES	
6. VOCATION	12. MAJORLEAGUEE	

SOLUTION TO PUZZLE 89: **The Final Frontier**

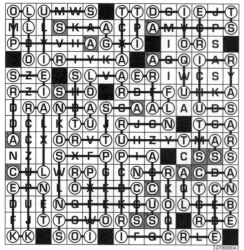

1. ARIES	7. SCORPIO	13. CAPRICORN
2. CLARKKENT	8. APOLLO	14. ALBERT
3. STARS	9. AQUARIUS	15. SUNSPOTS
4. SOLARFLARE	10. ASTRONAUTS	Scramble: CASSINI
5. SATURN	11. CANCER	
6. SAGITTARIUS	12. ASTEROID	

SOLUTION TO PUZZLE 90

1. OPERNHAUS	7. HORSEFEATHER	13. MALANG
2. HANGZHOU	8. HIGHSIGN	14. MICROMANAGERS
3. MAKWA	9. MARDELPLATA	Scramble: OFFENBACH
4. OYSTERSTEW	10. OXFORD	
5. OPENSOURCE	11. MARSHALL	
6. HERZEGOVINA	12. HOOVER	

SOLUTION TO PUZZLE 91: **The Human Body**

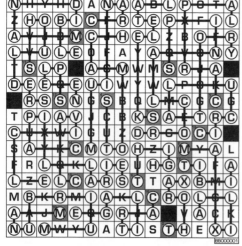

1. CRANIUM	7. SPINALCORD	13. CIRCULATORY
2. MAXILLA	8. THIGH	14. CAPILLARIES
3. THORAX	9. MANDIBLE	15. CLAVICLE
4. STOMACH	10. MANUBRIUM	16. CARTILAGE
5. CARPAL	11. SHOULDERS	17. SPLEEN
6. SKELETAL	12. TIBIA	Scramble: METATARSAL

SOLUTION TO PUZZLE 92

1. LLAMA	7. LIMIT	13. YELLOWJACKET
2. YESORNO	8. YEARNED	14. LASHOUT
3. VENERATE	9. VERACRUZ	15. VALUES
4. UPHOLSTER	10. UNSURPASSED	16. VERMICELLI
5. YOGURT	11. LASVEGAS	Scramble: UMBRELLAS
6. UZBEKISTAN	12. LIONSSHARE	

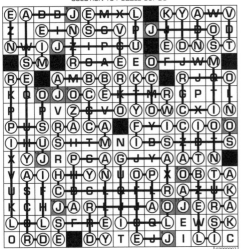

1. JULESVERNE
2. OBELISK
3. JOSTVANDYKE
4. JEOPARDY
5. OMICRON
6. OCCAMSRAZOR
7. JABBERWOCKY
8. JASMINE
9. OLIGARCHY
10. JUILLIARD
11. JAKARTA
12. OSPREY
13. OSSIFICATION
14. JAPANESE
Scramble: OPTICNERVE

1. LESOTHO
2. NETMAN
3. MEXICALI
4. NIAMEY
5. LUBUMBASHI
6. NAIROBI
7. LAUSANNE
8. MAMOUTZOU
9. NOVOSIBIRSK
10. MASERU
11. LARKSPUR
12. LJUBLJANA
13. LIFEFORCE
14. LITHUANIA
15. NOUAKCHOTT
Scramble: MOLDOVA

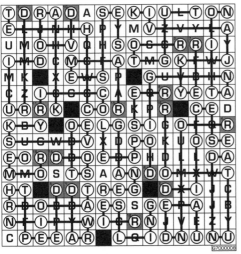

1. DARWIN
2. DIOCESE
3. ROTGUT
4. RONDEAU
5. DEEPTHROAT
6. DRUID
7. REYKJAVIK
8. RESIGNATION
9. DOPPELGANGER
10. DVORAK
11. RICOCHET
12. RIESLING
13. RAMESSES
14. DOSTOEVSKY
15. ROMEO
16. ROTUNDA
Scramble: DAMASCUS

1. KAOHSIUNG
2. KRASNOYARSK
3. MISSSAIGON
4. MAURITIUS
5. EARHART
6. ELEONORA
7. KIBOSH
8. MONKEES
9. MAMOUTZOU
10. ELMERGANTRY
11. MEDICO
12. KIPPERED
13. KEENEST
14. MARDELPLATA
15. EASTTIMOR
16. ENDEH
Scramble: ELONGATE

For Mendi,
My one and only, the Love of my life.